S0-AIX-431

THE RESTFUL IN MUSIC

THE RESTFUL IN MUSIC

by

Edward B. Benjamin, Sr.

SOLE U.S. DISTRIBUTOR
CRESCENDO PUB. CO.
48-50 MELROSE ST.
BOSTON, MASS. 02116

Copyright © 1970 by Edward B. Benjamin, Sr.
All rights reserved, no part of this book may be
reproduced in any form, or by any electronic or
mechanical means, including information storage and
rebound systems without permission in writing from
the publisher, except by a reviewer who may quote
brief passages in a review.

First Edition

Printed in the United States of America

ML
156.2
. B43

CONTENTS

THE RESTFUL IN MUSIC

Introduction

Nearly thirty years have gone by since I began my research on the restful in music, and undertook its implementation.

The intervening time has now been sufficient both for testing the validity of the concept, and building up the necessary repertoire.

The reason for the project was a very simple one: I needed soft, background music for over-time work when fatigue had already set in and such work was unavoidable.

What follows will tell how the project developed and the nature of the music resulting from it, — lovely and relaxing. In fact, if I were denied most of life's pleasures but had some choice in the matter, one of the joys retained would be this restful genre.

It is difficult to exaggerate the potential in the medium, and the utility inherent for the busy adult. Restful music can add up to a new dimension in living.

Furthermore, as will be related, even the person with broadest musical experience can find in the genre novel facets of composition, and opportunity for extended appreciation thereof.

Millions of Americans resent the incessant yowling and howling of jazz, bebop and rock n'roll. Millions more recoil from popular television programs or have no time for them. There are other millions still who do not relax fully in the home. In fact, we Americans often knock ourselves out with our diversions.

Restful music can help to overcome such conditions, and add to a person's efficiency and accomplishment.

* * *

CHAPTER ONE

Background

At the turn of the century before the advent of phonograph, radio and television in the home, people spelled music with a capital "C" for Culture, even more so than today.

My well-to-do father and mother[1] were no exceptions to this. But, additionally, they loved music, believed in it, and had considerable talent. As a result, most musical advantages were mine from early childhood.

An account will amuse or provoke you, dependent upon your attitude toward such indulgence.

With our old French Opera House the center of New Orleans' social and musical life and my parents habitués of the place, attendance began for me at the age of five.

Opera went on at home likewise. In one of my earliest childhood memories, I recall Mother at the piano playing and singing Puccini's Bohême, with Father sketching in the male roles. This opera had struck that more dramatically inclined generation with the impact of "South Pacific" or "The King and I," in our day.

My seventh year found me a budding cellist. For some time afterwards, Tannhauser's "Evening Star" proved a feature of school exercises, and with good reason: the solo instrument, the cello, was bigger than the performer.

At the mature age of eleven, came carte blanche both for opera attendance and purchase of any and all phonograph records. A friend of mine, a youngster from one of New York's wealthiest families[2], had a collection near our summer place that included one rendition of every number in the entire

---

1 The late Emanuel V. and Rachel G. Benjamin
2 The late Willard E. Loeb, whose mother was a Guggenheim.

Victor Red Seal catalogue. It is not too much to say that at fifteen the pair of us had become habitués of the opera house, with access additionally to most of the best recorded music in existence.

Oddly enough, here were boys who collected the musical greats along with tennis champions, baseball stars and football heroes, and were fairly good at sports themselves.

My mother having taken a hand in the founding of the New Orleans Philharmonic Society, the agency responsible for our concert seasons, it was only natural for an interest in other forms of music to accompany that for the operatic.

College days up East extended advantages further. By my twentieth year, I had written for the Harvard Musical Review, played in Harvard's Pierian Sodality[3] and attended a hundred concerts of the Boston Symphony, aided in my enjoyment of these by Phillip Hale's invaluable program notes.

Residence in an Eastern college also brought ready access to the Metropolitan Opera, where Toscanini, Hertz, and Bodanzski then conducted, and European travel furthered musical experience of all kinds.

Those were the days of the greats: Paderewski, Ysaÿe, Casals, Kreisler, Heifetz, Barrere, the irreplacable Caruso, Melba, Scotti, Amato, Matzenauer, Farrar, Homer, Barrientos, Bori, Ponselle — these and others almost equally illustrious, occupied the stages of concert hall and opera house, and dwafted many who followed.

Perhaps with my own interest encouraging them a bit, Mother and our good friend, Mrs. Andrew Stewart, organized a New Orleans Symphony in 1920, with Dr. Ernest Schuyten as conductor. This organization attracted an audience of only five or six hundred in a city of operatic tradition, and had to be discontinued after two or three years. But wanting symphony nonetheless, my father and I then founded, in 1923, the New Orleans Symphony Season, that brought down the St. Louis and Minneapolis Orchestras for nine concerts a year. This Season drew an attendance of only 1200, and was merged with

---

[3] Our country's oldest symphonic organization.

the New Orleans Philharmonic Society, my wife becoming first Vice President of that organization.

Eventually, the New Orleans Philharmonic Society merged with our present New Orleans Symphony, which was formed in 1936, my sister, Lucy Benjamin Lemann, taking a leading hand in this, although dividing her time between New Orleans and New York.

Mrs. Benjamin became a Vice President of the Philharmonic-Symphony, and our family interest has helped to bring the Orchestra along to a high ranking in the nation's musical life.

Lucy founded our Summer Pops.

A liking for chamber music brought me many hearings of such exponents as the Flonzaley Quartet and the Kneisels, including the latter's marvelous finale in Boston.

The Flonzaley, judged the world's best at the time, played its second to last concert in our New Orleans home.

Such, in brief, was my early musical background.

I am presently a Vice President of the New Orleans Opera House Association and honorary President of the Community Concert Association of New Orleans with its 4,000 subscribers. And I took the lead in organizing, and served as first President of the Cultural Attractions Fund of Greater New Orleans, designed to raise the annual deficit money for the city's ten major private cultural and artistic agencies, including opera, symphony, jazz, "Pops," etc.

Mrs. Benjamin continues to serve as a vice-president of the New Orleans Philharmonic Symphony.

Thus we retain a place in the musical life of New Orleans, meanwhile taking in much of the best abroad on our annual sojourns there.

CHAPTER TWO

Interest in the Restful

My specific interest in restful music came about through two accidents, one a happy circumstance, the other the greatest of tragedies — war.

Some time in my twenties, I lost interest in the phonograph — two much mechanics, too small a repertoire.

In the latter connection, childhood experience with such early record issues as the Beethoven Fifth and the Schubert Unfinished had taught that any music can be rendered banal through repetition.

In 1940, my son, Mente, brought to my attention new phonograph equipment with a scratch suppressor and other marked improvements, which had been installed at his preparatory school.

About the same time, an encyclopedia of recorded music came to hand, revealing the enormous, almost unbelievable growth in repertoire, that had taken place over the preceding fifteen or twenty years.

Having longed for additional musical facilities in the home, I wasted no time in ordering the necessary installations, and in building up a kind of record collection constituting a musician's dream: one that omits the commonplace, but explores the whole gamut of music from the ancients to the most advanced moderns.

And then came World War II. With my older sons and only brother in the armed services, anxieties mounted. Responsibilities, always considerable, just about doubled. Gradually there came over me a genuine craving for some relaxing influence in the home of evenings, particularly on so-called rest nights, when invariably reports and papers had to be looked over that could

4

not be covered in the daily, wartime grind.

In those days radio produced mainly blare. My record collection, with its thousands of titles, held much to intrigue. However, in periods of stress and fatigue, the dramatic no longer attracted to the same extent as before. The times and exigencies demanded the restful.

To my astonishment, even a varied and extensive collection offered only a modicum of such music. A slow movement could be obtained from a symphony here, another from a quartet there. But to put these together for a relaxing evening meant work. In the 78 rpm days, record sides and movements did not necessarily coincide. Furthermore, when LP's came in, no mechanics existed for stopping production between bands and isolating the more soothing sections.

This recognition of need for specific kinds of music to suit given mood or condition, led me to write an article on the use of the phonograph in the home, published in *ETUDE* (May, 1946), which the editor entitled "Building a Library of Records."

The writing likened music to food, pointing out that no composition existed, which could be called "good music" for all occasions. Instead, various kinds were good, in the sense of useful, dependent on mood or need.

In other words, there were and are times for such forms as the dramatic, the gay, the tranquil and cheerful, the restful and soothing.

More and more the realization dawned on me that in my life at the moment, the greatest need was for the last mentioned form. First, here was music most difficult of all to come by. And second, adults were bound to require this genre, especially as the years went by. Because, aside from overwork and fatigue, who does not encounter other factors in life, which call for anything and everything that can soothe and relax?

CHAPTER THREE

Definition and Evaluation

Meanwhile, I had been experimenting with the different forms and schools of composition, in an effort to define the genre most soothing and relaxing for the normal individual.

Think of floating on limpid water in the gathering twilight of a summer afternoon and early evening. Or imagine reclining in a wooded glade with the pipes of Pan played softly and slowly in the distance. Those were the effects desired for a restful medium, as I thought of it.

Some of my searching in this direction produced rather unexpected results. Quite obviously, to charm and soothe, the genre should be soft, slow and lovely. But there came the realization on close analysis that such music was not suitable if highly melodic — the tune would seize the attention and prevent complete relaxation.

Thoroughly analyzed, vocal works proved distracting, even *sotto voce,* because of one's unconscious tendency to seek out words.

Then came the finding that the piano did not relax, showering pellets of sound at a person as it does. And *pizzicato* effects of any kind had the same result.

Surprising as this may seem, it appeared that dissonance could soothe. Take, for example, the first part of the Largo in the Shostakovich Fifth: pitched high on the staff, here is music out of the world, sound that leads a person into a sort of stratospheric twilight, timeless in its consolation and beauty.

Following all such leads, gradually there evolved this definition of the restful in music: lovely, soft, slow composition, in either conventional or modern idiom, without vocal or marked percussive effect, and without obtrusive melody.

And although you may be inclined to feel that even normal people differ considerably in their reactions to sound, experience has proved the validity of the definition as stated, for most persons.

Musically erudite house guests confirmed this validity at once. But the final judgments were to come from unexpected quarters.

As an instance, shortly after the restful genre began to be produced in my New Orleans home, our French Provencale upstairs-maid demanded to know, "What eez thees musique? What eez eet? Eet eez bew-tiful!"

A week or so afterwards, the night watchman on the block apologized for intruding into a living room following his hourly call to headquarters, and exclaimed, "Boss, I had me a band back home in Tennessee, but I ain't never heard no music like this! What *is* this here music?"

As stated earlier, it would be impossible to exaggerate the beauty and usefulness of the genre. With it the home becomes a chapel. One walks in beauty, one breathes beauty, one lives in beauty. Nerves are soothed. Cares tend to disappear. Chores become less burdensome. And a fellow comes close to paradise with a loved one at his side to share such an experience.

In effect the music adds a dimension to human living in this sense: it is as if one had discovered sailing, skiing, the pleasure of the saddle, or some other delightful new sensation.

The restful repertoire yields exquisite satisfaction to attentive listening, and this could not be otherwise, for here in sequence is much of the more poetic musical inspiration through the centuries. But such composition is amply rewarding even listened to with one ear: the sound filters through pages of reports or journals and yields the little treat that overcomes the tedium of these assignments.

It is even possible for two or three persons to talk quietly with this background behind the conversation.

Probably no other musical genre offers so wide a range of enjoyment. Its utility extends beyond the home to public places of one kind or another — hospitals and other institutions, professional offices, conveyances — any and all environments where the soothing and restful can play a part.

CHAPTER IV

Provision for Restful Music

Once the restful genre had been defined, the stumbling block to enjoyment was its scarcity. Entirely aside from the phonograph, my ken of music brought little of the restful to mind. This was the realization that prompted me to begin a series of awards for such composition at Eastman School of Music of the University of Rochester, also awards and then commissions through the North Carolina Symphony. The idea appealed much to Dr. Howard Hanson at Eastman, with his great good sense and remarkable musicianship, as well as to Dr. Benjamin Swalin of the North Carolina Symphony, another fine and highly intelligent musician.

From the start, these awards and commissions produced beautiful, appropriate music, which has been publicly performed and privately recorded to build up the repertoire.

Sample titles tell their own story: through Eastman, "Christ Looking Over Jerusalem" (William Pursell), "For Katherine in April" (Ron Nelson), "In Memorian, Abraham" (Robert Stern)[3]; through the North Carolina Symphony, "Adagietto" (Theron Kirk), "Farewell" (Frederick Schreiber), "Nocturne for Orchestra in F Minor" (Gerhard Wuensch), "Scologue" (John Cook), "Fantasy for Orchestra" (Jan Schinhan), "Symphony No. 6 — Celestrial Gate" (Alan Hovhaness), "Poem for Peace" (Thad Jones).

But gradually the realization dawned on me that an hour or two of new composition each year would hardly suffice to provide for a lifetime's enjoyment.

Shortly after this, lovely Mrs. Richard Weingart of New York and Nassau, recommended to me an able young musicol-

---

[3] Mercury MG-50053 includes the three Eastman award compositions mentioned and others.

ogist, Walter Diehl, formerly a program editor at The New York Times' WQXR and later program director of another good New York music station, WAFB.

I then engaged Walter to research the entire serious repertoire of music on phonograph records for the selection of numbers answering my requirements.

WQXR gave us permission to use its vast library of records, the largest this side of the Atlantic. Walter spent months at WQXR and elsewhere, monitoring and listing to my specifications. The result was a catalogue of restful music that comprised nearly a thousand titles.

This catalogue has been revised constantly to add suitable numbers as they emanated on new recordings. When Walter Diehl could no longer give time to the research, Mr. Eugene Showalter, formerly a professional oboist with the New Orleans Symphony, took over and continued the research for me, monitoring all new record releases that offered promise.

The restful music research titles are set forth later, in alphabetical order by composers.

Some selections may sound more tranquil than restful, that is they may charm and cheer, rather than charm and soothe. But most of this music fits into the desired genre, although one must remember that very little composition has been written for specifically restful purposes.

An occasional number may be found that is neither restful nor tranquil to the listener. This is entirely understandable considering the extent of the listings and variance in human taste. Also, "boys will be boys," and Walter and Eugene slipped in a few numbers they thought might be educational for me. In turn, I have not had the heart to strike out the works, considering the dedication of these research men to their task.

Many of the compositions can be obtained in two or more recordings. The listings may not necessarily reflect the best performances, but they will be found acceptable in almost every instance.

Most of this music has been transferred to tapes[4] for my

---

4 The taping has been done by Walter Diehl and Eugene Showalter as part of their research.

homes, providing a restful repertoire about two hundred hours in duration, with nearly two thousand titles.

Reels can be played in either direction. With ten-inch tapes, this adds up to an hour and forty-five minutes of uninterrupted enjoyment from each track.

Composers range from the earliest classicists, many of them barely known, to such moderns as Schonberg, Prokofiev, Bartok, Shostakovich, Honegger, Copland, and to some others thought quite extreme. A little, at any rate, has been gleaned from very unlikely sources — the listings can broaden musical knowledge for just about everyone.

The tapes alternate the classical, romantic and modern, reducing any tendency toward monotony, and providing an artistic mix as well.

My original awards at Eastman and through the North Carolina Symphony, were extended shortly afterwards to include Juilliard School of Music. Additionally, Mr. Eugene Ormandy of the Philadelphia Orchestra, an old friend, recommended a number of composers for restful commissions: Richard Yardumian, Louis Gesenway, Dr. Eugene Zador, Miklos Rozsa, Gottfried von Einen, Nicholas Nabokov, and Virgil Thomson. The resulting compositions have been premiered by the Philadelphia.

Nadia Boulanger, conducting the New York Philharmonic February 15th to 18th, 1962, premiered the transcription for symphony of Virgil Thomson's "A Solemn Music," commissioned by me as a part of the larger restful score for the Philadelphia's 1962-63 season.

Among other composers who received my awards or commissions for restful composition, were Chester V. J. Anderson, Richard Arnell, Wayne Barlow, Jack Behrens, Dr. John Boda, Romeo Cascarino, Donald Cervone, Ramiro Cortes, M. Thomas Cousins, Paul Creston, Emma Lou Diemer, Arthur De Nero, Paul Earls, George Faust, Lukas Foss, Vincent Frohne, Robert Fauldin, T. Ritter George, Philip Glass, Louis B. Gordon, Dr. Howard Hanson, Dr. Herbert Hazelman, Peggy Glanville Hicks, Dorothy Hill, Jack Jarrett, Hunter Johnson, James Johnson, Ulysses Kay, James Kurtz, Melvin Lucas, Martin Mailman,

Dr. Wilton Mason, Neil McKay, Louis Mennini, Haruna Milyake, Ken Murley, Theodore S. Newman, Bernard Rogers, Robert Rohe, Gunther Schuller, Joseph Scianna, Michael Smolonoff, Willard Straight, James L. Sutcliffe, Conrad Susa, Dr. Benjamin F. Swalin, Robert Ward, Brett Watson, Maurice Weeks, Hershel White, John White, Michael White, Stephen Wieldsznski, Clifton Williams, David Williams, and Ramon Zupko.

The award and commission works have given pleasure already to many and encouraged the production of more music of the kind.

Among enthusiasts was the late Olin Downes, probably the dean of American music critics in his day. After auditioning for so many years, and becoming bored or irritated by some of the experimental sound effects passing for music, Mr. Downes got particular pleasure from a genre that charmed and soothed.

In an effort to encourage more composition of real merit, Mr. Downes suggested to me through the late Alexander Hilsberg[5], an annual award or commission for tranquil composition, a genre that could charm and cheer. This has evoked such works as William Cameron White's "Elegy," Paul Nordoff's "Little Symphony," Paul Creston's "Ancient Dances," Howard Hanson's "Summer Seascape," and Romeo Cascarino's "Divertimento for Woodwinds, Horns, Strings, Harp, Celeste and Percussion – The Cajun Country." Virgil Thomson also received the tranquil commission for his orchestral transcription of the Brahms "Preludes and Fugues," which has been performed by the Philadelphia, Boston and Berlin Philharmonic symphonies, among others.

There has been a good deal of publicity about the restful music project and the tranquil commissions, with articles in TIME, NEWSWEEK, HARPER'S, HOUSE BEAUTIFUL, HI-FI, just about all the musical magazines and the daily press of this and other nations, as well.

As a result, nearly a thousand requests have come in for the restful listings from all over this country and abroad. Presumably, many others are now producing such music, privately

---

[5] Conductor of the New Orleans Symphony at the time, and until shortly before his death in 1961.

and publicly.

The restful listings were immediately made available, gratis, to the recording companies and RCA promptly came forth with a platter, the Stokowski "Restful (Good) Music" album[6], consisting of the following selections:

SIDE ONE

Cesti	TU MANCAVI A TORMENTARMI, CRUDELISSIMA
Frescobaldi	GAGLIARDA
Lully	Le Triomphe de l'Amour: NOCTURNO
Purcell	Dido and Aeneas – WHEN I AM LAID IN EARTH
J. S. Bach	MEIN JESU (Symphonic transcriptions by Stokowski)

SIDE TWO

J. S. Bach	SICILIANO (from Sonata for Violin and Cambalo in C Minor
J. S. Bach	Suite No. 2, in B Minor, Third Movement: SARABANDE
Beethoven	Symphony No. 6, in F, Opus 68 ("Pastoral")
	Second Movement: SCENE BY THE BROOKSIDE
	Members of the NBC Symphony Orchestra
Bizet	L'Arlesienne Suite No. 1 Third Movement: ADAGIETTO

People who bought it were genuinely enthusiastic about this record. Some played it over and over – a practice that would probably spoil an album for anyone with a very musical ear. But these patrons continued to love the program, nonetheless.

Mercury has recorded under the title "Music for Quiet Listening"[7] some of the Eastman restful award compositions, truly beautiful works that belie the youth of the students who wrote them. This was the album used over the national networks in the Jack Kennedy obsequies.

Columbia now has a Yardumian album which includes "Veni, Sancet Spiritus," one of the commissioned works, performed by Mr. Ormandy and the Philadelphia (mono. ML-5629 stereo MS-6229).

But, facing up to facts, quite obviously recording companies cannot be depended upon to reproduce numbers fulfilling the restful criteria already on platters or tapes, because obviously

---

[6] Victor LM-1875
[7] Mercury MG-50053   MS-90053

again it pays better to bring out six Beethoven quartets, let us say, than the slow movements from each of these quartets. And very few works are restful as a whole. It is as simple as that.

Some radio stations are beginning to broadcast restful music[8], but most take the position that their function is to stimulate rather than to soothe. Even the authorities at WQXR feel this way for all their public spirit, the station depending to some extent on advertising revenues, as do its lesser rivals.

Moreover, there is an astonishing lack of understanding in radio regarding the appropriateness of musical genres for different occasions. Most of the higher-minded stations feel that "good music" has an over-riding virtue of its own, any time and for any and all purposes, which simply is not so. To illustrate: how many people want the dramatic at 10:30 in the evening or during the dinner hour? Or, going to the other extreme, how many really want unceasing rock and roll for hours on end?

Surely, in music as elsewhere, there is a time and place for everything.

A few orthodox critics have tended to decry the inclusion of isolated movements from larger works in the restful repertoire, on the theory that this breaches artistic integrity. In my opinion, the attitude is responsible in part for good music becoming a charitable cause. The art has been placed on a pedestal by devotees, although it does not add up to a sanctity, a religion, or even an education.

In the 17th and 18th centuries musicians ate with the servants. Today the common man looks to music merely for enjoyment. As between such viewpoints and deification of music, there should be some happy medium. Treating music as functional in nature and using it for restful among other purposes, represents a step in this direction.

In present day living, so-called popular "mood" discs dispense a good deal of soothing comfort to those millions who are not sufficiently musical to be distracted by melody.

At one time following the publicity given my restful music

---

8 The British Broadcasting Corporation has instituted two restful programs weekly.

project, forty per cent of the record output was in that medium.

This popular output and the restful repertoire covered herein, are both highly useful for their individual purposes.

Taking all the above into account, it may be necessary for the serious seeker after the restful to put his own repertoire together on tape. With the listings available herein, that can be done more easily than might be imagined, using records and picking up restful movements from radio broadcasts, both permissible courses for the individual to pursue in his own home.

But a person can urge a local station to provide a restful hour from the research listings, which has brought results in some instances.

We talk a great deal about music as an international medium of expression and amity. The restful genre would lend itself particularly well for these purposes. My address brought this out when the University of Rochester awarded me an honorary doctorate in October, 1960, during a convocation on "Perspectives for Peace."

The restful repertoire cannot be recommended too highly to one and all for such use as may be indicated in their daily living, even by those who do not consider themselves "musical."

Rare indeed is the individual who would not respond to the beauty and the peace offered by the music considered herein. This writing has been undertaken with that thought in mind.

THE LISTINGS

ALBINONI, TOMMASO (1674-1745)

Adagio for Organ and Strings
    Ensemble Instrumental Sinfonio, Jean Witold, cond.
    Period 723

Concerto a Cinque in A minor, Opus 5, No. 5   Mvt. II
    Jean-Francois Paillard Chamber Orchestra
    Musical Hertiage Society MHS-552

Concerto a Cinque, Opus 9
    No. 2 in D Minor for Oboe: Mvt. II
    No. 3 in F Major for Two Oboes: Mvt. II
    No. 5 in C Major for Oboe: Mvt. II
    No. 6 in G Major for Two Oboes: Mvt. II
    No. 9 in C Major for Two Oboes: Mvt. II
    No. 10 in F Major for Violin: Mvt. II
    No. 12 in D Major for Two Oboes: Mvt. II
    Ferraresi, violin; Visai and Milanesi, oboes
    Italian Baroque Ensemble, Vittorio Bryks, cond.
    3 Vox DL-193

Concerto in B Flat Major, Opus 7, No. 3:   Mvt. II
    Pierre Peirlot, oboe
    Antiqua Musica Chamber Orch. Jacques Rousell, cond.
    Angel 36325

Concerto in B Flat for Oboe, Opus 7, No. 3:   Mvt. II
    Andre Lardrot, oboe
    Vienna Opera Chamber Orchestra, Felix Prohaska
    Vanguard 1025   stereo 2036

Concerto in C Major for Oboe, Opus 7, No. 12:   Mvt. II
    Pierre Pierlot, oboe
    Oiseau-Lyre Orchestral Ensemble, Louis de Froment, cond.
    Oiseau-Lyre OL-50041

Concerto in D Minor, Opus 5, No. 7:   Mvt. II
    Italian Chamber Orchestra, Newell Jenkins, cond.
    Haydn Society 9027

Concerto in D Minor, Opus 9, No. 2:   Mvt. II
    Pierre Pierlot, oboe
    Antiqua Musica Chamber Orch., Jacques Rousell, cond.
    Angel 36325

Concerto in D Major for Oboe, Opus 7, No. 6:   Mvt. II
    Renato Zanfini, oboe
    Virtuosi di Roma, Renato Fasano, cond.
    Angel 45019

Concerto in D Major, Opus 7, No. 6:   Mvt. II
    Pierre Pierlot, oboe
    Antiqua Musica Chamber Orch., Jacques Roussel, cond.
    Angel 36325

Concerto in F Major, Opus 7, No. 9:   Mvt. II
    Pierre Pierlot, oboe
    Antiqua Musica Chamber Orch., Jacques Roussell, cond.
    Angel 36325

Concerto in G for Flute;   Mvt. II
    Jean-Francois Paillard Chamber Orch.
    Musical Heritage Society MHS-552

Concerto for Violin in D Major, Opus 9, No. 7:   Mvt. II
    Pellicia, Virtuosi di Roma, Renato Fasano, cond.
    Decca 9598

Sonata for Strings in G Minor, Opus 2, No. 6: Mvts. I, III
    Virtuosi di Roma, Renato Fasano, cond.
    Decca 9572

ALBINONI, TOMMASO (Cont.)

Trio Sonata in A, Opus 1, No. 3: Mvts. I, III
Societas Musica of Copenhagen
Bach Guild BG-566

ALFVEN, HUGO (1872-1960)

Gustav Adolf II Suite: Elegy
Stockholm Concert Assoc. Orchestra, Grevillius, cond.
Victor album M-788 (78 rpm)

Symphony No. 3 in E Flat Major: Mvt. II
Stockholm Concert Assoc. Orchestra, Alfven, cond.
His Master's Voice DB-11026/9 (78 rpm)

ALPAERTS, FLOR (1876-1954)

James Ensor Suite: Mvt. III, "The Garden of Love"
Belgian National Orchestra, Louis Weemaels, cond.
London LL-874

ANTHEIL, GEORGE (1900-1959)

Serenade No. 1 for Strings: Mvt. II
Oslo Philharmonic, Alfredo Antonini, cond.
Composers Recordings, Inc. CRI-103

ARENSKY, ANTON (1861-1906)

Variations on a Theme by Tchaikovsky
I. Moderato
II. Allegro non troppo
III. Andantino tranquillo
V. Andante
VII. Andante con moto
VIII. Coda: Moderato
Kapp Sinfonietta Strings, Emanuel Vardi, cond.
Kapp 9059

ARNOLD, MALCOLM (1921-   )

Homage To The Queen: Air
Philharmonia Orchestra, Robert Irving, cond.
Victor LM-2037

Four Scottish Dances: No. 3
London Philharmonic, Arnold, Cond.
Everest 6021   Stereo 3021

Symphony No. 2, Opus 40: Mvt. III
Royal Philharmonic Orchestra, Arnold, cond.
Epic LC-3422

Sinfonietta: Mvts. i, II
Northern Sinfonia Orch., B. Brott, cond.
Mace (s) 9068

ARRIAGA, JUAN CRISTOSOMO (1806-1826)

Quartet No. 1 for Strings in D Minor: Mvt. II
Guilet String Quartet
Concert Hall Society H-1508

Symphony in D Major: Mvt. II
Orquesta de Conciertos de Madrid, Arambarri, cond.
Columbia ML-5464 Stereo MS-6134

ARRAUXO, F. C. de (c. 1581 - unknown)

Tres Glosas sobre el Canto Llano de la Immaculada Concepcion
Helmuth Riling, Stuttgard Memorial Church Organ
Turnabout TV-4097

ATTERBERG, KURT (1887-   )

Suite Pastorale, Opus 34: Mvt. II
    Chamber Orchestra conducted by Atterberg
    His Master's Voice X-4966/7 (78 rpm)

Symphony No. 6 in C Major, Opus 31: Mvt. II
    Royal Philharmonic Orchestra, Beecham, cond.
    Columbia album M-279 (78rpm)

BACH, CARL PHILIPP EMANUEL (1714-1788)

Adagio in D Minor
    Carl Weinrich, organ
    Victor LM-2793

Concerto No. 3 for Cello in A Major: Mvt. II
    Andre Navarra, cello
    Orchestra conducted by André Cluytens
    English Columbia LX-8819/21 (78 rpm)

Concerto in D Minor for Flute: Mvt. II
    Kurt Redel, flute
    Munich Pro Arte Orch., Kurt Redel, cond.
    Decca DL-10092

Concerto for Flute in G Major: Mvt. II
    Jean-Pierre Rampal, flute
    Oiseau-Lyre Orchestral Ensemble, Louis de Froment, cond.
    Oiseau-Lyre OL-50121

Flute Sonata in B Flat Major: Mvt. I
    Rampal, flute; Veyron-Lacroix, harpsichord
    Nonesuch H-1034

Concerto for Oboe in E Flat: Mvt. II
    Haydn Sinfonietta. Hans Kempler, cond.
    Ermanno Tosti, oboe
    Baroque BU-1819

Concerto for Orchestra in D Major: Mvt. II
    MGM Chamber Orchestra, Izler Solomon, cond.
    MGM E-3109

Concerto for Orchestra in D Major: Mvt. II
    The Philadelphia Orchestra, Eugene Ormandy, cond.
    Columbia MS-6342

Concerto for Organ and Orchestra in E Flat Major: Mvt. II
    Marie-Claire Allain, organ
    Leclair Instrumental Ensemble, Paillard, cond.
    Westminster 18754

Concerto for Four Viols: Mvt. II
    Ensemble Marius Casadesus
    Westminster 18130

Duo in E Minor for Flute and Violin: Mvt. I
    Kurt Redel, flute
    Ulrich Grehling, violin
    Oiseau-Lyre OL-50017

Quartet in G Major (Wq. 95): Mvt. II
    Pohlers, flute; Schmid, viola;
    Buhl, cello; Galling, harpsichord
    VOX DL 463-1 Stereo STDL-500463

Sinfonia in B Minor: Mvt. II
    Mainz Chamber Orchestra, Kehr, cond.
    VOX DL 463-1

Sinfonia No. 5 in B Minor: Mvt. II
    Mainz Chamber Orchestra, Gunter Kehr, cond.
    VOX PL-14070

BACH, CARL PHILLIP EMANUEL (Cont.)

Sinfonia No. 3 in C Major: Mvt. II
    Vienna Symphony Orchestra, Felix Guenther, cond.
    Bach Guild 504

Sonata No. 4 in D Major: Mvt. I
Sonata No. 5 in G Major: Mvt. I
    Jean-Pierre Rampal, flute
    Veyron-Lacroix, harpsichord
    Nonesuch H-1034 stereo 71034

Sonata in G Minor (2 variations)
    Piguet, baroque oboe
    Odyssey 32 16 0050

Symphony No. 2 in B Flat: Mvt. II
    The Paillard Chamber Orchestra
    Musical Heritage Society MHS 549

Trio in B Minor for Flute, Violin & Continuo: Mvt. II
    Kurt Redel, Ulrich Grehling, Imgard Lechner
    Oiseau-Lyre OL-50017

Trio for Flute in B Minor (Wq. 143): Mvt. II
    Pohlers, flute; Kehr, violin;
    Buhl, cello; Galling, harpsichord
    Vox DL 463-1 stereo STDL-500463

Trio in E Major: Mvt. II
    Ars Rediviva Ensemble of Prague
    Parliament PLPS 619

BACH, JOHANN CHRISTIAN (1735-1782)

Concerto for Cello in C Minor: Mvt. II
    Joseph Schuster, cello
    Los Angeles Orchestra Society, Franz Waxman, cond.
    Capitol P-8232

Concerto for Flute in D: Mvt. II
    Amadeo Pucci, flute
    Haydn Sinfonietta. Hans Kempler, cond.
    Baroque BU-1819

Quartet for Flute, Violin, Viola and Cello: Mvt. II
    Helmut Riessberger, flute
    Momoo Kishibe, violin
    Hatto Bayerle, viola
    Wilfried Boettcher, cello
    Musical Heritage Society 545

Sinfonia in B Flat Major, Opus 18, No. 2: Mvt. II
    Louis de Froment Chamber Orchestra
    Angel 35338

Sinfonia in E Flat Major, Op. 9, No. 2: Mvt. II
    Munich Pro Arte Orchestra, Kurt Redel, cond.
    Decca DL-10092

Sinfonia in D Major, Opus 18, No. 3: Mvt. II
    Concert Hall Symphony Orchestra, Van den Berg, cond.
    Concert Hall Society G-3

Sinfonia Concertante in E Flat Major: Mvt. II
    Vienna Symphony Orchestra, Felix Guenther, cond.
    Bach Guild 504

Sinfonia for Double Orchestra in D Major, Opus 18, No. 3, Mvt. II
    The Philadelphia Orchestra, Eugene Ormandy, cond.
    Columbia MS-6342

Sinfonia for Double Orchestra in E Flat Major: Mvt. II
    The Philadelphia Orchestra, Eugene Ormandy, cond.
    Columbia ML-5580 stereo MS-6180

BACH, JOHANN CHRISTIAN (Cont.)

Symphony No. 2 in B Flat: Mvt. II
    Eichendorf Wind Group
    Musical Heritage Society MHS-581

Symphony in G Minor: Mvt. II
    Saar Chamber Orchestra. Karl Ristenpart, cond.
    Music Guild M-14

Three Instrumental Pieces from "Amadis:" First Piece
    Zimbler Sinfonietta. Richard Burgin, cond.
    Boston B-405

BACH, JOHANN SEBASTIAN (1685-1750)

Aria (from Organ Pastorale in F Major) arr. Casals
    Pablo Casals, cello
    Perpignan Festival Orchestra
    Columbia ML-4926

Art of The Fugue: Contrapunctus IV
                    Contrapunctus XVIIIa
    MGM String Orchestra, Arthur Winograd, cond.
    MGM 2 E 3

Brandenburg Concerti No. 1 in F Major: Mvt. II
                    No. 2 in F Major: Mvt. II
                    No. 4 in G Major: Mvt. II
                    No. 6 in B Flat Major: Mvt. II
    Stuttgart Chamber Orchestra, Karl Munchinger, cond.
    3 London CMA-7211   Stereo CSA-2301

Cantata No. 21 "Ich hatte viel Bekuemmernis:" Sinfonia
    Pforsheim Chamber Orch. Fritz Werner, cond.
    Musical Heritage Society MHS 527

Chorale: Ach, Gott vom Himmel Sieh'Darein (arr. McDonald)
    The Philadelphia Orchestra, Eugene Ormandy, cond.
    Columbia ML-5065

Chorale: My Jesus in Gethsemane (arr. Stokowski)
    Leopold Stokowski and Orchestra
    Victor LM-1875*

Chorale: My Soul is Athirst (arr. Stokowski)
    The Philadelphia Symphony, Leopold Stokowski, cond.
    Victor album M-401 (78 rpm)

Chorale Prelude: I Call To Thee (arr. Stokowski)
    The Philadelphia Symphony, Leopold Stokowski, cond.
    Victor 11-8577 (78 rpm)

Chorale Preludes: Glory Be To God in the Highest (BWV 662)
                    Before Thy Throne I Now Appear (BWV 662)
                    From God Shall Nought Divide Me (BWV 658)
                    Come, Holy Ghost (BWV 658)
    Marie-Clair Alain, organ
    Musical Heritage Society MHS 643

Chorale Preludes: Savior of The Heathen, Come
                    All Praise to Jesus' Hallowed Name
                    Now Praise We Christ, The Holy One
                    The Old Year Now Hath Passed Away
                    Lamb of God, Our Savior
                    When On The Cross The Savior Hung
                    O Man. Bewail Thy Grievous Fall

———

*Restful Good Music album

21

BACH, JOHANN SEBASTIAN (Cont.)

Blessed Jesus, At Thy Word
I Call To Thee, Lord Jesus Christ
When In The Hour of Utmost Need
Herman Walcha, organ
Archive 3025/6

Come, Sweet Death (arr. Ormancy)
The Philadelphia Orchestra, Eugene Ormandy, cond.
Columbia ML-5065

Concerto in A Minor for Flute, Violin and Harpsichord
(BWV 1044): Mvt. II
Granville Jones, violin
Philomusica of London, Thurston Dart, cond.
Oiseau Lyre OL-60007

Concerto in D Minor (after Vivaldi): Mvt. II
E. Power Biggs, organ
Columbia ML-4500

Concerto for Oboe d'Amore in A Minor — Larghetto
Leon Goossens, oboe d'amore
Philharmonia Orchestra, Walter Susskind, cond.
Columbia ML-4782

Concerto for Oboe in F Major (BWV 1053): Mvt. II
Helmut Winschermann, oboe
Deutsche Bacholisten
Cantate 057-701

Concerto No. 1 for Violin in A Minor: Mvt. II
Isaac Stern, violin
The Philadelphia Orchestra, Eugene Ormandy, cond.
Columbia ML-5087

Concerto No. 2 for Violin in E Major: Mvt. II
Szymon Goldberg, violin
Philharmonic String Orchestra, Walter Süsskind, cond.
Decca DL 7507

Concerto for Violin, Oboe and Orchestra in C Minor: Mvt. II
Isaac Stern, violin; Marcel Tabuteau, oboe
Prades Festival Orchestra, Pablo Casals, cond.
Columbia ML-4351

Concerto for Two Violins and Orchestra in D Minor: Mvt. II
Isaac Stern and Alexander Schneider, violins
Prades Festival Orchestra, Pablo Casals, cond.
Columbia ML-4351

Fantasia in C Major (arr. Bedell)
Arthur Fielder Sinfonietta
Victor 13809 (78 rpm)

German Organ Mass: Gott Vater in Ewigkeit
Vater unser im Himmelreich
Christ unser Herr, zum Jordan kam
Fritz Heitmann, organ
Capitol P-8029

Italian Concerto (arranged for orchestra) Mvt. II
Berlin Philharmonic, Hans Schmidt-Isserstedt, cond.
Capitol L-8128

Musical Offering: Trio Sonata: Mvts. I and III
Ricercare a 6
Ricercare a 8
Stuttgart Chamber Orchestra, Munchinger, cond.
London LL-1181

BACH, JOHANN SEBASTIAN (Cont.)

Preludes (3) from "The Well-Tempered Cavalier" (trans. Villa-Lobos)
The Violoncello Society, Heitor Villa-Lobos, cond.
Everest 6024 stereo 3024

Siciliano (from Sonata for Violin and Cembalo in C Minor)
arranged by Stokowski
Leopold Stokowski and orchestra
Victor LM-1875*

Sinfonia from Cantata 12
Sinfonia from Cantata 21
Harry Shulman, oboe
Orchestra directed by Daniel Saidenberg
Kapp 9041 stereo S-9041

Sinfonia from Cantata 106
Vienna Chamber Orchestra, Hermann Scherchen, cond.
Westminster 18394

Sinfonia to Cantata 106 ("Actus Tragicus")
Pforsheim Chamber Orchestra, Werner, cond.
Musical Heritage Society MHS-628

Sinfonia from Cantata 147 - "Jesus, Joy of Man's Desiring"
arranged by Stokowski
Leopold Stokowski and orchestra
Victor LM-1176

Sinfonia ("Arioso") from Cantata 156
Harry Shulman, oboe
Orchestra directed by Daniel Saidenberg
Kapp 9041 Stereo S-9041

Sinfonia from Cantata 208 - "Sheep May Safely Graze"
arranged by Stokowski
Leopold Stokowski and Orchestra
Victor LM-1877

Sinfonia from The Christmas Oratorio, "Shepherd's Song"
Leopold Stokowski and Orchestra
Capitol P-8489

Sinfonia from the Easter Oratorio (arr. Whittaker)
Leon Goossens, oboe
Liverpool Philharmonic, Sir Malcolm Sargent, Cond.
Columbia ML-4782

Sonata in C Minor (BWV 1033): Mvt. III
Jean-Pierre Rampal, flute
Robert Veyron-Lacroix, harpsichord

Sonata in E Minor (BWV 1034): Mvt. III
Sonata in E Major (BWV 1035): Mvt. III
Jean-Pierre Rampal, flute
Robert Veyron-Lacroix, harpsichord
Jean Huchot, cello
Epic SC-6045

Sonata in C Major (from BWV 1037): Mvts. I and II
Philomusica of London. Thurston Dart, cond.
Oiseau Lyre PL-60007

Sonata in E Minor BWV 1023): Mvt. II
Reinhold Barchet, violin
Robert Veyron-Lacroix, harpsichord
Jacoba Muckel. cello
Musical Heritage Society MHS-628

----

*Restful Good Music Album

BACH, JOHANN SEBASTIAN (Cont.)

Sonata in A Minor for Flute Unaccompanied: Mvt. II
  Jean-Pierre Rampal, flute
  Epic SC-6045

Sonata for Flute in A Major (BWV 1034): Mvt. II
Sonata for Flute in G Minor (BWV 1020): Mvt. II
  Jean-Pierre Rampal, flute
  Robert Veyron-Lacroix, harpsichord
  Epic SC-6045

Sonata in B Minor for Flute: Mvt. II
Sonata in E Flat for Flute: Mvt. II
  Jena-Pierre Rampal, flute
  Robert Veyron Lacroix, harpsichord
  Epic SC-6045

Sonata in C Minor for Violin (BWV 1024): Mvt. III
Sonata in F Major for Violin (BWV 1022): Mvts. I and III
  Reinhold Barchet, violin
  Robert Veyron-Lacroix, harpsichord
  Jacoba Muckel, cello
  Musical Heritage Society MHS-628

Sonata No. 3 for Violin and Cembalo (arr. Bachrich): Mvt. III
  Arthur Fiedler Sinfonietta
  Victor 13809 (78 rpm)

Suite No. 2, in B Minor: Mvt. III
  Leopold Stokowski and his Symphony Orchestra
  Victor LM-1875*

Suite No. 3 for Orchestra: Mvt. II
  Stuttgart Chamber Orchestra, Karl Munchinger, cond.
  London CM-9072

Tocatta, Adagio and Fugue in C Major: Adagio
  transcribed by Eugene Ormandy
  The Philadelphia Orchestra, Ormandy, cond.
  Columbia ML-5580   stereo MS-6180

Trio Sonatas: No. 1 in E Flat Major: Mvt. II
          No. 2 in C Minor: Mvt. II
          No. 3 in D Minor: Mvt. II
          No. 4 in E Minor: Mvt. II
          No. 5 in C Major: Mvt. II
          No. 6 in G Major: Mvt. II
  Helmut Walcha, organ
  Archive ARC-3013/3014

Trio Sonata No. 1 in C Major: Mvts. I, III
  Claude Monteux, flute; Harry Shulman, oboe,
  George Ricci, cello; Robert Conant, harpsichord
  American Society AS-1004

Trio Sonata in D Minor (BWV 1036): Mvts. I, III
  Rudolph Kalup and Thomas Kakushka, violins
  Anatal Tichy, cello; Hilde Langfort, harpsichord
  Musical Heritage Society MHS-654

Trio Sonata in G Major (BWV 1038): Mvts. I, III
  Helmut Riessberger, Gernot Kury, flutes
  Rudolph Kalup, violin; Hilde Langfort, harpsichord
  Musical Heritage Society MHS-654

Trio Sonata in G Major (BWV 1039): Mvt. III
  The Ars Rediviva Ensemble of Prague
  Parliament PLPS 619

*Restful Good Music album

BACH–WALTON

The Wise Virgins (ballet suite): Mvts. II, III, V
Vienna State Opera Orchestra, Franz Litschauer, cond.
Vanguard 440

BACH, WILHELM FRIEDEMANN (1710-1784)

Concerto for Harpsichord in E Flat: Mvt. II
Zimbler Sinfonietta. Richard Burgin, cond.
Boston B-404

Sinfonia in D Minor: Mvt. I
Louis de Froment Chamber Orchestra
Angel 35338

BADINGS, HENK (1907–   )

Symphony No. 7 ("Louisville"): Mvt. III
The Louisville Orchestra, Robert Whitney, cond.
Louisville LOU-566

BALAKIREV, MILI (1837-1910)

Symphony No. 1 in C Major: Mvt. III
Royal Philharmonic Orchestra, Beecham, cond.
Angel 35399

BANKS, DON (arranger) (1923-   )

Elizabethan Miniatures: The Irish Ho-Hoane
Sinfonia of London. Robert Irving, cond.
Odeon CLP-1571

BARANOVICH, KRESHIMIR (1894-   )

The Gingerbread Heart: Episode
Belgrade Philharmonic, Baranovich, cond.
London LL-1235

BARBER, SAMUEL (1910-   )

Adagio for Strings (from Quartet in D Major)
Boston Symphony Orchestra, Charles Munch, cond.
Victor LM-2105

Concerto for Cello and Orchestra: Mvt. II
Zara Nelsova, cello
New Symphony Orchestra, Barber, cond.
London LPS-332

Concerto for Violin and Orchestra, Opus 14: Mvt. II
Wolfgang Stavonhagen, violin
Imperial Philharmonic, William Strickland, cond.
Composers Recordings, Inc. CRI-137

Medea, Opus 23 (ballet suite): Mvts. IV and VI
New Symphony Orchestra, Barber, cond.
London CM-9145

Serenade for Strings, Opus 1: Mvt. II
Symphony of the Air, Vladimir Golschmann, cond.
Vanguard VRS-1065 Stereo VSD-2083

Summer Music, Opus 13
The Philadelphia Woodwind Quintet
Columbia ML-5441 stereo MS 6114

Symphony No. 2, Opus 19: Mvt. II
New Symphony Orchestra, Barber, cond.
London CM-9145

BARLOW, WAYNE (1912-   )

Rhapsody for Oboe, "The Winter's Past"
Robert Sprenkle, oboe
Eastman-Rochester Symphony, Howard Hanson, cond.
Mercury MG-50076

Night Song
Eastman-Rochester Symphony, Howard Hanson, cond.
Mercury MG-50277

BARSANTI, FRANCESCO (c.1690-c.1760)

Concerto Grosso in D Minor, Opus 3, No. 4: Mvt. IV
Lamoureux Chamber Orchestra, Pierre Colombo, cond.
Oiseau-Lyre OL-50008

Concerto for Two Horns in D Major: Mvt. II
Stagliano and Berv, Horns
Kapp Sinfonietta, Richard Dunn, cond.
Kapp 9053

BARTOK, BELA (1881-1945)

Concerto for Violin and Orchestra (1938): Mvt. II
Tibor Varga, violin
Berlin Philharmonic Orchestra, Ferenc Fricsay, cond.
Decca 9545

Dance Suite (1923): Mvt. I
New Symphony Orchestra, Franco Autori, cond.
Bartok 302

Hungarian Sketches: "Evening in the Village"
                       "Melody"
Minneapolis Symphony Orchestra, Antal Dorati, cond.
Mercury MG-50132   stereo 90132

Quartet No. 1 for Strings: Mvt. I
Ramor String Quartet
Vox VBX-19   stereo SVBX-519

Quartet No. 5 for Strings: Mvt. II
Juilliard String Quartet
Columbia ML-4280

Sonata for Unaccompanied Violin: Melodia
Ivry Gitlis, violin
Dover HCR-5211

Suite No. 2 for Orchestra: Mvt. III
Minneapolis Symphony Orchestra, Antal Dorati, cond.
Mercury MG-50098   stereo 90098

Two Images for Orchestra: "In Full Flower"
New Symphony Orchestra, Tibor Serly, cond.
Bartok 307

Two Portraits for Orchestra: "The Idealist"
Jean Pougnet, violin
New Symphony Orchestra, Franco Autori, cond.
Bartok 303

BAX, ARNOLD (1883-1953)

Symphony No. 3: Lento
The Halle Orchestra, John Barbirolli, cond.
His Master's Voice G-3380/5 (78 rpm)

BEETHOVEN, LUDWIG VAN (1770-1827)

Duo No. 2 for Clarinet and Bassoon: Mvt. II
di Dario and Cimonelli
Classic Editions 1013

Egmont: Incidental Music, Opus 84 - "Entr-acte No. 2"
"Klarchens Tod"
SW German Radio Symphony, Eduard van Remoortel
VOX PL-10870 stereo STPL-510870

Octet in E Flat Major, Opus 103: Mvt. II
Vienna Philharmonic Wind Group
Westminster 18189

Quartet in C Major (after Piano Sonata, Opus 2, No. 3): Mvt. II
Pascal String Quartet
Concert Hall Society 1201

Quartet in F Major (after Piano Sonata, Opus 14, No. 1): Mvt. II
New Music String Quartet
Bartok 909

Quartet No. 2 in G Major, Opus 18, No. 2: Mvt. II
Budapest String Quartet
Columbia ML-5393 stereo MS-6074

Quartet No. 3 in D Major, Opus 18, No. 3: Mvt. II
Budapest String Quartet
Columbia ML-5394 stereo MS-6095

Quartet No. 6 in B Flat Major, Opus 18, No. 6: Mvt. II
Budapest String Quartet
Columbia ML-5395

Quartet No. 8 in E Minor, Opus 59, No. 2: Mvt. II
Budapest String Quartet
Columbia ML-5586

Quartet No. 10 in E Flat Major, Opus 74: Mvt. II
Budapest String Quartet
Columbia ML-5588

Quartet No. 11 in F Minor, Opus 95: Mvt. II
Kroll String Quartet
Epic LC-3779

Quartet No. 12 in E Flat Major, Opus 127: Mvt. II
Hollywood String Quartet
Capitol P-8443

Quartet No. 13 in B Flat Major, Opus 130: Mvt. V
Budapest String Quartet
Columbia ML-4584

Quartet No. 13 in B Flat Major, Opus 130: Mvt. V
arranged for Orchestra:
Berlin Philharmonic Orchestra, Wilhelm Furtwängler
Capitol-Telefunken H-8130

Quartet No. 14 in C Sharp Minor, Opus 131: Mvts. I and IV
Budapest String Quartet
Columbia ML-4585

Quartet No. 15 in A Minor, Opus 132: Mvt. III
Budapest String Quartet
Columbia ML-4586

Quartet No. 16 in F Major, Opus 135: Mvt. III
Budapest String Quartet
Columbia ML-4587

Quartet No. 16 in F Major, Opus 135: Mvt. III
arranged for Orchestra:
NBC Symphony Orchestra, Toscanini, cond.
Victor LCT-1041

27

BEETHOVEN, LUDWIG VAN (Cont.)

Quintet for Strings in C Major, Opus 29: Mvt. II
Barylli Quartet; Hübner, viola
Westminster 18409

Romance No. 1 in G Major for Violin and Orchestra
Romance No. 2 in F Major for Violin and Orchestra
Igor Oistrakh, violin
Leipzig Gewandhaus Orchestra, Franz Konwitschny, cond.
Decca 9875

Septet in E Flat Major, Opus 20: Mvt. II
NBC Symphony Orchestra, Toscanini, cond.
Victor LM-1745

Sextet in E Flat Major, Opus 71: Mvt. II
Vienna Philharmonic Wind Group
Westminster 18189

Sonata in B Flat, Opus 106 — "Hammerklavier:" Mvt. III
arranged by Weingartner
Bavarian Symphony Orchestra, Kurt Graunke, cond.
Urania 7089

Symphony No. 1 in C Major, Opus 21: Mvt. II
Orchestre de la Suisse Romande, Ernest Ansermet
London CM-9162   stereo CS-6120

Symphony No. 4 in B Flat Major, Opus 60: Mvt. II
London Philharmonic Orchestra, Georg Solti, cond.
Richmond 19033

Symphony No. 6 in F Major, Opus 68: Mvt. II
Leopold Stokowski and his Symphony Orchestra
RCA Victor LM-1875*

Symphony No. 9 in D Minor, Opus 125: Mvt. III
NBC Symphony Orchestra, Toscanini, cond.
Victor LM-6009

Trio for Strings in E Flat Major, Opus 3: Mvt. IV
Jean Pougnet, Frederick Riddle, Anthony Pini
Westminster 18410

Trio for Strings in D Major, Opus 8: Mvt. II
Jean Pougnet, Frederick Riddle, Anthony Pini
Westminster 18412

Trio for Strings in G Major, Opus 9, No. 1: Mvt. II
Jean Pougnet, Frederick Riddle, Anthony Pini
Westminster 18411

Trio for Two Oboes and English Horn, Opus 87: Mvt. II
Kamesch, Kautsky, Hadamousky
Westminster 18409

BELLINI, VINCENZO (1801-1835)

Oboe Concerto in E Flat Major: Mvt. II
Pierlot, oboe
J. F. Paillard Chamber Orchestra
Musical Heritage Society MHS-595

BENDA, FRANZ (1709-1786)

Trio Sonata in E Major: Mvts. I and II
David and Igor Oistrakh, violins
Waldimir Yampolski, piano
Helidor H-25009

_____

*Restful Good Music Album

BENDA, JIRI ANTONIN (or GEORG) (1722-1795)
Symphony in B Flat for Strings: Mvt. II
    Czech Philharmonic, Vaclav Tálich, cond.
    Supraphone MAB-2

Symphony in C Major: Mvt. II
Symphony in E Flat Major: Mvt. II
Symphony in F Major: Mvt. II
Symphony in G Major: Mvt. II
    Musici Prgaenses, Libor Hlavacek, cond.
    Crossroads 22 16 0059   stereo 22 16 0060

BEN-HAIM, PAUL (1897-   )
Concerto for String Orchestra, Opus 40: Mvt. III
    MGM String Orchestra, Izler Solomon, cond.
    MGM 3423

BEREZOWSKY, NICOLAI (1900-1953)
Suite for Wind Quintet, Opus 11: Mvts. II and IV
    New Art Quintet
    Classic Editions 1003

BERGSMA, WILLIAM (1921-   )
Gold and Senor Commandante: "Siesta"
                                    "Tender Dance"
    Eastman-Rochester Symphony Orchestra, Howard Hanson, cond.
    Mercury MG-50147

Quartet No. 2 for Strings: Mvt. III
    Walden String Quartet
    Desto D-425

Quartet No. 3 for Strings: Mvt. III
    Juilliard String Quartet
    Columbia ML-5476

BERKELEY, LENNOX (1903-   )
Divertimento in B Flat Major: Mvt. II
    London Chamber Orchestra, Anthony Bernard, cond.
    Decca AK-1882/3 (78rpm)

Serenade for Strings: Mvt. II and IV
    Stuttgart Chamber Orchestra, Karl Munchinger, cond.
    London LL-1395

Trio for Strings in C Major, Opus 19: Mvt. II
    Jean Pougnet, Frederick Riddle, Anthony Pini
    Westminster 18515

BERLINSKI, HERMAN (1910-   )
Symphonic Visions for Orchestra: Mvt. II
    Asahi Orchestra of Tokyo, Richard Korn, cond.
    Composers Recordings, Inc. CRI-115

BERLIOZ, HECTOR (1803-1869)
Dance of the Sylphs, from "The Damnation of Faust"
    The Philadelphia Orchestra, Eugene Ormandy, cond.
    Columbia ML-5261

Romeo and Juliet: "Love Scene"
    Boston Symphony Orchestra, Charles Munch, cond.
    Victor LM-1988

BERNERS, LORD (1883-1950)
The Triumph of Neptune: "The Frozen Forest"
    Royal Philharmonic, Sir Thomas Beechan, cond.
    Columbia ML-4593

BERNSTEIN, LEONARD (1918-   )
Serenade for Violin, Strings and Percussion: Mvt. IV
Isaac Stern, Symphony of the Air, Bernstein
Columbia ML-5144

BERWALD, FRANZ (1796-1868)
Symphony in C Major: Mvt. II
Symphony in G Minor: Mvt. II
Stockholm Philharmonic Symphony. Schmidt-Issersted, cond.
Nonesuch H-1087   stereo 71087

BESOZZI, CARLO (1738—Unknown)
Sonata XX for Two Oboes, Two Horns, and Two Bassoons: Mvt. II
Eichendorf Wind Group
Musical Heritage Society MHS-581

BIBER, HEINRICH VON (1644-1704)
Balletti Lamentabili: Lamento, Allemande, Sarabande
and Lamento
Concentus Musicus
Bach Guild BG-652

Serenada: Air
Prague Pro Arte Antiqua Consort of Viols
Bach Guild 591   stereo S-5019

Sonata IV (Fidicinium Sacro-Profanum) Mvts. I and II
Leonhart Consort
Telefunken AWT 9461

BINET, JEAN (1893-   )
String Quartet: Mvt. II
Swiss String Quartet
London LL-498

BIZET, GEORGES (1838-1875)
L'Arlesienne Suite No. 1: Mvt. III
Leopold Stokowski and his Symphony Orchestra
Victor LM-1875*

Fair Maid of Perth, Suite: Serenade No. 1
Paris Conservatory Orchestra, Edouard Lindenberg, cond.
London LL-871

BLACKWOOD, EASLEY (1933-   )
Symphony No. 1: Mvts. II, IV
Boston Symphony Orchestra, Charles Munch, cond.
Victor LSC-2352

BLAVET, MICHEL (1700-1768)
Sonata for Flute No. 6 in A Minor: Mvts. I, III
Rampal, flute
Veyron-Lacroix, harpsichord
Dover HCR-5238   stereo 7238

BLISS, ARTHUR (1891-   )
A Colour Symphony: Mvt. III
London Symphony Orchestra, Bliss, cond.
London LL-1402

Miracle In The Gorbals: Mvt. V and VII
The Philharmonic Orchestra, Bliss, cond.
Angel 35136

----

*Restful Good Music Album

BLISS, ARTHUR (Cont.)

Music For Strings: Mvt. II
    The Philharmonia Orchestra, Bliss, cond.
    Angel 35136

Quartet No. 2 for Strings in F Minor: Mvt. II
    Griller String Quartet
    London LL-1550

Quintet for Clarinet and Strings: Mvt. III
    Gervase de Peyer, clarinet
    Melos Ensemble of London
    Everest 3135

Quintet for Oboe and Strings: Mvt. I
    Peter Graeme, oboe
    Melos Ensemble of London
    Everest 3135

BLOCH, ERNEST (1880-1959)

Concerto for Violin: Mvt. II
    Joseph Szigeti, violin
    Paris Conservatory Orchestra, Charles Munch, cond.
    Columbia ML-4679

Four Episodes for Piano, Wind and Strings: Mvt. III "Calm"
    Knickerbocker Chamber Players, Izler Solomon, cond.
    MGM 3245

Meditation and Processional: Mvt. I (meditation)
    Paul Doktor, viola
    Marylin Mason, organ
    Mirrosonic RM-1013

Night
    Griller String Quartet
    English Decca album 93 (78 rpm)

Quartet No. 1 for Strings in B Minor: Mvt. III
    Roth String Quartet
    Mercury MG-50110

Quartet No. 2 for Strings: Mvt. III
    Musical Arts Quartet
    Vanguard 437

Quartet No. 5 for Strings: Mvts. I, II
    Fine Arts Quartet
    Concert Disc M-1225   stereo 225

Sinfonia Breve: Mvts. II, IV
    Minneapolis Symphony Orchestra, Antal Dorati
    Mercury MG-50288

Trois Poèmes Juifs: Mvt. II (Rite-in part)
    Hartford Symphony Orchestra, Mahler, cond.
    Vanguard 2085

Voice In The Wilderness: Mvts. II, IV
    Zara Nelsova, cello
    London Philharmonic Orchestra, Ernest Ansermet, cond.
    London CM-9133

BLOW, JOHN (1649-1708)

Venus and Adonis (Suite for Strings): Second Act Tune
           The Graces Dance
           Sarabande for the Graces
           Third Act Tune
    Oiseau-Lyre Chamber Orchestra, Anthony Lewis, cond.
    Oiseau-Lyre OL-50004

BOCCHERINI, LUIGI (1734-1805)

Concerto for Cello in B Flat Major: Mvt. II
Pierre Fournier, cello
Stuttgart Chamber Orchestra, Karl Münchinger, cond.
London CM-9104

Concerto for Cello in D Major, Opus 34: Mvt. LL
August Wenzinger, cello
Schola Cantorum Basiliensis, Joseph Bopp, cond.
Archive 3057

Quartet for Strings in A Major, Opus 39, No. 3: Mvt. III
Quartetto Italiano
Angel 35062

Quartet for Strings in B Flat Major, Opus 1, No. 2: Mvt. II
New Music String Quartet
Columbia ML-5047

Quartet for Strings in D Major, Opus 6, No. 1: Mvt. II
Quartetto Italiano
London LL-320

Quartet for Strings in E Flat Major, Opus 58, No. 2: Mvt. II
New Music String Quartet
Columbia ML-5047

Quartet for Strings in E Flat Major, Opus 58, No. 3: Mvt. II
Quartetto Italiano
Angel 35062

Quintet in E Major, Opus 13, No. 5: Mvt. I
Alexander Schneider Quintet
Vanguard VRS-1147   stereo 71147

Quintet in F Major, Opus 20, No. 4: Mvt. II
Stradivari Quintet
Musical Heritage MHS 645

Quintet for Flute and Strings in E Flat Major: Mvt. I
Richard Adeney, flute
London Baroque Ensemble, Karl Hass, cond.
Westminster 18050

Quintet for Guitar and Strings in D Major: Mvt. II
Karl Scheit, guitar
Vienna Konzerthaus Quartet
Vanguard 1044

Quintet for Strings in A Minor, Opus 10, No. 1: Mvt. II
Quintetto Boccherini
Angel 45007

Quintet for Strings in A Minor, Opus 47, No. 1: Mvt. III
Günter Kehr and Wolfgang Bartels, violins
Erich Sichermann and Volker Kirchner, violas
Bernard Braunholz, cello
Turnabout TV 4094

Quintet for Strings in A Major, Opus 29, No. 6: Mvt. III
Quintetto Boccherini
Angel 45010

Quintet for Strings in C Minor, Opus 18, No. 5: Mvt. II
Quintetto Boccherini
Angel 45011

Quintet for Strings in C Minor, Opus 29, No. 1: Mvt. II
Quintetto Boccherini
Angel 45008

Quintet for Strings in C Major, Opus 25, No. 3: Mvt. II
Quintetto Boccherini
Angel 45010

BOCCHERINI, LUIGI (Cont.)

Quintet for Strings in C Major: Mvt. III
   The Stradivari Quartet, Harvy Shapiro
   Musical Heritage Soceity MHS 694

Quintet for Strings in D Minor, Opus 41: Grave
   Quintetto Boccherini
   Angel 45007

Quintet for Strings in D Major, Opus 18, No. 5: Mvt. II
   Quintetto Boccherini
   Angel 45011

Quintet for Strings in F Major, Opus 13, No. 3: Mvt. II
   Quintetto Boccherini
   Angel 45009

Quintet for Strings in F Major, Opus 41, No. 2: Mvt. II
   Quintetto Boccherini
   Angel 45006

Quintet for Strings in G Major, Opus 60, No. 5: Mvt. III
   Quintetto Boccherini
   Angel 45008

Sextet for Strings in E Flat Major, Opus 24, No. 1: Mvt. II
   London Baroque Ensemble, Karl Haas, cond.
   Westminster 18051

Serenade in D Major: Mvt. V
   Haifa Symphony, Sergiu Comissiona, cond.
   Mace MS-9051

Sinfonia in C Major, Opus 16, No. 3: Mvt. II
   Vienna Orchestral Society, F. Charles Adler, cond.
   Unicorn 1017

Symphonies from Opus 21:
   No. 1 in B Flat Major: Mvt. II
   No. 3 in C Major: Mvt. II
   No. 5 in B Flat Major: Mvt. II
   No. 6 in A Major: Mvt. II
   Austrian Tonkuenstler Orchestra, Lee Schaenen, cond.
   Musical Heritage Society MHS 651

Symphony in C Minor: Mvt. II
   Guiseppe Prencipe, solo violin
   Rossini di Napoli Orchestra, Franco Caracciolo, cond.
   London CM-9445   stereo 6445

Trio for Strings, Opus 35:
   No. 1 in F Major: Mvt. I
   No. 2 in G Major: Mvt. III
   No. 3 in E Major: Mvt. II
   No. 5 in C Major: Mvt. I
   No. 6 in E Major: Mvt. II
   Schneiderhan, Swoboda, Benesch
   Westminster 18050/52

Trio for Strings, Opus 14:
   No. 4 in D Major: Mvt. II
   No. 5 in E Flat Major: Mvt. I
   The New York String Trio
   Dover HCR 7007

BOCCHERINI—FRANCAIX

Scuola di Ballo: Pastorale
   London Philharmonic, Antal Dorati, cond.
   Entre R L-3043

BODINUS, SEBASTIAN (Last Half of 18th Century)

Trio in E Flat Major: Mvt. III
Berlin Camerata Musicale
Nonesuch H-70185

BODLYE, SEOIRSE (1933-)

Music for Strings: Mvt. II
Radio Eireann Symphony Orchestra, Milan Horvat, cond.
Decca 9843

BOHM, GEORG (1661-1733)

Chorale Prelude "Vater Unser"
Hans Heintze.
Archive 3037

BOISMORTIER, JOSEPH BONDIN DE (1691-1755)

Concerti (2) for Five Flutes: Slow Movements
Dufrene, Rochut, Rampal, Kenvyn, Lussagnet
Anthologie Sonore 159 (78 rpm)

Concerto for Five Flutes in D Major: Mvt. II
Helmut Riessberger, Gernot Kury,
Herbert Reznicek, Johann Futschik,
Gerhard Perz
Musical Heritage Society MHS 574

Concerto in E Minor for Five Instruments, Opus 37: Mvt. II
Leclair Instrumental Ensemble, J. F. Paillard, cond.
Haydn Society 103

Concerto in B Minor, Opus 21, No. 4: Mvt. II
Maxence Larrieu Instrumental Quartet
Musical Heritage Society MHS-CC2

Daphnis et Chloe: Air, Louré
Chamber Orchestra, Emil Seiler, cond.
Helidor HS 25018

Gentillesse ("La Racine")
Philomusica of London, Thurston Dart, cond.
Oiseau-Lyre 50174

Sonata in E Minor, Opus 37, No. 2: Adagio
Maxence Larrieu Instrumental Quartet
Musical Heritage Society MHS-CC2

Sonata in G Minor, Opus 34, No. 1: Mvt. I
Maxence Larrieu Instrumental Quartet
Musical Heritage Society MHS-CC2

Sonata for Two Flutes: Mvts. I, IV
Dufrene and Rochut
Anthologie Sonore 157 (78 rpm)

Sonata for Three Flutes: Mvt. I
Dufrene, Rochut, Lussagnet
Anthologie Sonore 158

Sonata for Three Flutes in D Major: Mvt. II
Helmut Riessberger, Gernot Jury
Herbert Reznicek
Musical Heritage Soceity MHS-574

Sonate pour les violons, Opus 34: Mvts. I, II
Orchestre de Chambre, Gerard Cartigny, cond.
Music Guild M-18 stereo (S) 106

BONDEVILLE, EMMANUEL (1898-)

Madame Bovary, Symphonic Suite: Mvt. III
Belgian National Orchestra, Georges Sebastian, cond.
London Int. 91023

BONPORTI, FRANCESCO (1672-1749)

Concerti a Quattro, Opus 11:
    No. 4 in B Flat Major: Mvt. II
    No. 5 in F Major: Mvt. II
    No. 6 in F Major: Mvt. II
    No. 8 in D Major: Mvt. II
    Roberto Michelucci, violin
    Enzo Altobelli, cello
    I Musici
    Epic LC-3541

BORODIN, ALEXANDER (1833-1887)

Symphony No. 1 in E Flat Major: Mvt. III
    Bavarian Symphony Orchestra, Kurt Graunke, cond.
    Urania 7066

BOYCE, WILLIAM (1710-1779)

Symphony No. 1 in B Flat Major: Mvt. II
Symphony No. 6 in F Major: Mvt. II
Symphony No. 7 in B Flat Major: Mvt. II
    Zimbler Sinfonietta
    2 Decca DX-105

BRAHMS, JOHANNES (1833-1897)

Chorale Preludes, Opus 122:
    Herzliebster Jesu
    O Welt, ich muss dich lassen (I)
    Schmücke dich, O liebe Seele
    O wie selig
    Es ist ein Ros' entsprungen
    Herzlich tut mich verlangen (II)
    Ernest White, Organ
    Mercury MG-10070

Chorale Prelude: Es ist ein Ros' entsprungen (arr. Leinsdorf)
    Cleveland Symphony Orchestra, Erich Leinsdorf, cond.
    Columbia album M-617 (78 rpm)

Concerto for Violin in D Major, Opus 77: Mvt. II
    Isaac Stern, violin
    Royal Philharmonic Orchestra, Sir Thomas Beecham, cond.
    Columbia ML-4530 stereo MS-6153

Concerto for Violin and Cello in A Minor, Opus 102: Mvt. II
    Jean Fournier, violin; Antonio Janigro, cello
    Westminster 18268

Quartet for Strings in C Minor, Opus 51, No. 1: Mvt. II
    Budapest String Quartet
    Columbia ML-4799

Quintet for Clarinet and Strings in B Minor, Opus 115: Mvt. II
    David Oppenheim, clarinet
    Budapest String Quartet
    Columbia ML-5626 stereo MS-6226

Serenade No. 1 in D Major, Opus 11: Mvts. III, IV
    Symphony of the Air, Leopold Stokowski, cond.
    Decca DL-10031 stereo (7) 10031

Serenade No. 2 in A Major: Adagio non troppo (in part)
    Hamburg Philharmonia, Arthur Winograd, cond.
    MGM E-3477

Sextet for Strings in G Major, Opus 36: Mvt. III
    Vienna Konzerthaus Quartet, Hübner, Weiss
    Westminster 18445

BRAHMS, JOHANNES (Cont.)

String Quintet in F Major, Opus 88: Mvt. II
Vienna Konzerthaus Quartet, Stangler 2nd viola
Westminster XWN-18063

Symphony No. 1 in C Minor, Opus 68: Mvt. II
Philharmonia Orchestra, Otto Klemperer, cond.
Angel 35481   stereo S-35481

Symphony No. 3 in F Major, Opus 90: Mvt. II
Philharmonia Orchestra, Otto Klemperer, cond.
Angel 35545   stereo S-35545

BRITTEN, BENJAMIN (1913-   )

Four Sea Interludes from "Peter Grimes:" Moonlight
Concertgebouw Orchestra of Amsterdam, Van Beinum, cond.
London LL-917

Quartet No. 1 for Strings in D Major: Mvt. II
Galimir String Quartet
Esoteric 504

Simple Symphony for Strings, Opus 4: Sarabande
New Symphony Orchestra, Eugene Goossens, cond.
London CM-9146

Sinfonia da Requiem, Opus 20 (1941)   Requiem Aeternam
St. Louis Symphony, Andre Previn, cond.
Columbia ML-5983   stereo MS-6583

Variations On A Theme by Frank Bridge, Op. 10 (1937):
Introduction
Adagio
Romance
Funeral March
Chant
Finale

Bath Festival Orchestra, Yehudi Menuhin, cond.
Angel 36303

BRUCH, MAX (1838-1920)

Canzone, Opus 55
Antonio Janigro, cello
London Philharmonic Symphony, Arthur Rodzinski, cond.
Westminster 18007   stereo - 14985

Concerto No. 1 for Violin in G Minor, Opus 26: Mvt. II
Ruggiero Ricci, violin
London Symphony Orchestra, Pierino Gamba, cond.
London CM-9194   Stereo CS-6010

Kol Nidrei for Cello and Orchestra, Opus 47
Antonio Janigro, cello
London Philharmonic Symphony, Arthur Rodzinski, cond.
Westminster 18007   stereo - 14985

Scottish Fantasy, Opus 46: Mvts. I, III
Michael Rabin, violin
Philharmonia Orchestra, Sir Adrian Boult, cond.
Angel 35484

BRUCKNER, ANTON (1824-1896)

Quintet for Strings in F Major: Mvt. II
Koeckert String Quartet, Schmid
Decca 9796

Symphony No. 2 in C Minor: Mvt. II
Linz Bruckner Orchestra, G. L. Jochum, cond.
Urania 402

BRUCKNER, ANTON (Cont.)

Symphony No. 3 in D Minor: Andante (in part)
Vienna Philharmonic, Hans Knappertsbusch, cond.
London CM-9107

Symphony No. 4 in E Flat Major: Andante quasi allegretto
Vienna Symphony, Otto Klemperer, cond.
Vox PL-11200

Symphony No. 5 in B Flat Major: Adagio
Vienna Philharmonic, Hans Knappertsbusch, cond.
London CM-7208 stereo CSA-2205

Symphony No. 6 in A Major: Mvt. II
Vienna Symphony Orchestra, Henry Swoboda, cond.
Westminster 18074

Symphony No. 7 in E Major: Mvt. II
Vienna Symphony, Willem Van Otterloo, cond.
Epic SC-6006

Symphony No. 9 in D Minor: Mvt. III
Amsterdam Concertgebouw, Eduard Van Beinum, cond.
Epic LC-3401

BRUNETTI, GAETANO (1740-1808)

Symphony in C Minor: Mvt. II
Italian Chamber Orchestra, Newell Jenkins, cond.
Haydn Society 9019

Symphony No. 22 in G Minor: Mvt. II
Italian Chamber Orchestra, Newell Jenkins, cond.
Haydn Society 9019

Symphony No. 23 in F Major: Mvt. II
Angelicum Orchestra of Milan, Newell Jenkins, cond.
Nonesuch H-71156

BULL, JOHN (c. 1562-1628)

In Nomine
The In Nomine Players
Vanguard-Bach Guild BG-576

BULL, OLE (1810-1880)

Saeterjentens Sondag
Oslo Philharmonic Orchestra
Mercury MG-10150

BUTTERWORTH, GEORGE (1885-1916)

A Shorpshire Lad
London Philharmonic Orchestra, Sir Adrian Boult, cond.
London LL-1169

BUXTEHUDE, DIETRICH (1637-1707)

Chorale Preludes: Nun komm, der Heiden Heiland
Ach Herr, mich armen Sünder
Jesus Christus, unser Heiland
Mensch, willt du leben seliglich
Nun bitten wir den Heiligen Geist
Von Gott will ich nicht lassen
Alf Linder, organ
Westminster 18507

Herr Jesu Christ, ich weiss gar wohl
Walter Kraft, organ
in Vox VXB-27

BUXTEHUDE, DIETRICH (Cont.)

Sonata in A Minor, Opus 1, No. 3: Slow Movements
Robert Brink, violin
Judith Davidoff, viola da gambe
Daniel Pinkham, harpsichord
Music Guild MG-121

BYRD, WILLIAM (1543-1623)

In Nomine
The Jaye Comsort of Viola. Grayston Burgess, cond.
Turnabout TV-4017

Miserere
Carl Weinrich, organ
Musicraft album 9 (78 rpm)

Pavane, "The Earl of Salisbury"
E. Power Biggs, organ
Columbia ML-4331

Pavane, "The Earl of Salisbury" — Instrumental version
The Philadelphia Symphony, Leopold Stokowski, cond.
Victor 1943 (78 rpm)

CABANILLES, JUAN BAUTISTA (1644-1712)

Tiento de "falsas"
Batalla Imperial (organ)
Achive ARC-73240

CABEZON, ANTONIO DE (1510-1566)

Variaciones sobre el canto del Caballero
Helmuth Rilling, Stuttgart Memorial Church Organ
Turnabout TV 4097

Diferencias Cavallero
Robert Noehren, organ of Kenmore
Presbyterian Church, Buffalo, N.Y.
Allegro LEG-9016

Variations sur le Chant de Chevalier and D'ou vient cela
Pierre Foidebise
Organ of Saint-Laurent d'Alkmaar
Nonesuch H-1016 stereo 71016

CAIX d'HERVELOIS, LOUIS DE (1670-1760

Suite in G for Cello and Harpsichord: Mvt. I, III
Le Rondeau de Paris
Nonesuch HC-73014

CAMBINI, GIOVANNI (1746-1825)

Quartet for Strings in D Major: Mvt. II
Quartetto di Roma
Victor album M-376 (78rpm)

CANNABICH, CHRISTIAN (1731-1798)

Minuetto
Stuttgart Viol. Trio
Janus 19013

Sinfonia No. 5 in B Flat: Mvt. II
Northern Sinfonia Orchestra, Broid Brott, cond.
MACE MCS-9096

Symphony in B Flat Major: Mvt. II
Berlin State Orchestra, Gmeindl, cond.
Deutsche Grammophon 69501/3 (78 rpm)

CANNING, THOMAS (1911-)
Fantasy on a Theme by Justin Morgan
Eastman-Rochester Orchestra, Howard Hanson, cond.
Mercury MG-50074

CARPENTER, JOHN ALDEN (1876-1951)
Adventures In A Perambulator: The Lake
Eastman-Rochester Orchestra, Howard Hanson, cond.
Mercury MG-50136 stereo 90136

CARREIRA, ANTONIO (XVI Cent.)
Fantasia in D Minor
E. Power Biggs, organ
Columbia KL-6167

CASELLA, ALFREDO (1883-1947)
Five Pieces for String Quartet: Nos. 2 and 4
New Music String Quartet
Bartok 906

Italia: Two excerpts
Symphony Orchestra of Radio Berlin, Rolf Kleinert, cond.
Urania UR-7118

La Giara: in part
Accademia di Santa Cecilia Orchestra, Previtali, cond.
London CM-9174 Stereo STS-15024

Serenade for Small Orchestra: Mvt. IV
Symphony Orchestra of Radio Leipzig, Herbert Kegel, cond.
Urania UR-7118

CASTELNUOVO-TEDESCO, MARIO (1895-)
Quintet for Guitar and Strings, Opus 143: Mvt. II
Andres Segovia, guitar
Quintetto Chigiano Strings
Decca 9832

CATALANI, ALFREDO (1854-1893)
Serenatella: A Sera
Scarlatti Orchestra of Naples, Pietro Argento, cond.
Colosseum 1040

CESTI, MARC ANTONIO (1623-1669)
Tu Mancavi a Tormentarmi (arr. Stokowski)
Leopold Stokowski and Orchestra
Victor LM-1875*

CHADWICK, GEORGE WHITEFIELD (1854-1931)
Symphonic Sketches: No. 2, "Noel"
Eastman-Rochester Orchestra, Howard Hanson, cond.
Mercury MG-50104 stereo 90018

CHARPENTIER, MARC-ANTONIE (1634-1704)
Concert for Viols: Prelude, Sarabande
Viols Quartet of the Schola Basiliensis
Musical Heritage Society MHS-598

Concert pour quatre parties: Mvts. II, V
Ensemble Instrumental, Andree Colson, cond.
VOX DL-630

----

*Restful Good Music Album

CHARPENIER, MARC-ANTONIE (Cont.)

Noels: Or dites-nous Marie
Ou s'en vont ces gays Bergers
A Createur
Leclair Instrumental Ensemble, Paillard, cond.
Musical Heritage Society MHS-570

CHAUSSON, ERNEST (1855-1899)

Poème de l'Amour et de la Mer, Opus 19: Interlude
London Philharmonic, Louis de Froment, cond.
London LL-1386
Poème for Violin and Orchestra, Opus 25
Aaron Rosand, violin
Southwest German Radio Orchestra, Rolf Reinhardt, cond.
VOX PL-10470
Viviane, Opus 5
Hamburg Philharmonia, Arthur Winograd, cond.
MGM 3434

CHEDEVILLE, NICOLAS (The Younger) (late 18th Cent.-Unknown)

Third Sonata in C Major for Two Flutes: Mvts. I, III, V
Helmut Riessberger, Gernot Kury, flutes
MHS-574

CIMA, GIOVANNI (16th-17th Cent.—exact dates unknown)

Sonata a tre, from Concerti ecclesiastici
Franco Gulli, Cesare Ferraresi, violins
Giacinto Caramia, cello
Achille Berruti, organ
Musica Sacra AMS-46

CIMAROSA, DOMENICO (1749-1801)

Concerto for Oboe (arr. Arthur Benjamin): Mvt. III
Leon Goossens, oboe
Liverpool Philharmonic, Sir Malcolm Sargent, cond.
Columbia ML-4782
La Cimarosiana (arr. Malipiero): Mvt. IV
Royal Opera House Orchestra, Warwick Braithwaite, cond.
MGM 3333

CIRRI, GIOVANNI BATTISTA (c.1740)

Concerto for Flute, Cello and Strings in A Major: Mvt. II
Tassinari, flute; Mazzacurati, cello
Virtuosi di Roma, Renato Fasano, cond.
Decca 9598
Four Centuries Suite: Prelude
Three Elizabeths Suite: Elizabeth of Glamis
New Symphony Orchestra, Eric Coates, cond.
London CM-9065

CLEMENTI, MUZIO (1752-1832)

Symphony in D Major: Mvt. II
Haifa Symphony, Sergiu Comissiona, cond.
Mace MS-9051

CLÉRAMBAULT, LOUIS NICOLAS (1676-1749)

Sonata "La Félicité:" Lent
Sonata "La Magnifique:" Mvts. I, III, IV
    Trio do Paris
    Soc. Francaise du Son SXL 20.139
Suite in the First Mode: Mvts. IV, VI
Suite in the Second Mode: Mvt. V
    Andre Marchal, Organ, Cathedral of Auch
    Musical Heritage SocietyMHS-640

COBERT, ROBERT (1924-   )

Mediterranean Suite: Mvt. I
    MGM Orchestra, Robert Cobert, cond.
    MGM 3497

COPERARIO, GIOVANNI (Unknown-1626)

Suite for Two Violins, Bass Viol and Chamber Organ
    Fantasy
    Alman
    Galliard
    Neville Marriner and Peter Gibbs, violins
    Desmond Dupre and Dennis Nesbitt, bass viols
    Thurston Dart, Chamber organ and harpsichord
    L'Oiseau Lyre O L-50133

COPLAND, AARON (1900-   )

Appalachian Spring (ballet Suite): Mvts. I, III, VI, VIII
    Boston Symphony Orchestra, Aaron Copland, cond.
    Victor LM-2401   stereo LSC-2401
Billy The Kid (ballet suite): Prairie Night
    The Philadelphia Orchestra, Eugene Ormandy, cond.
    Columbia ML-5157
Concerto for Clarinet and String Orchestra: Mvt. I
    Benny Goodman, clarinet
    Columbia String Orchestra, Aaron Copland, cond.
    Columbia ML-4421   stereo MS-6497
Our Town: The Story of Grover's Corners
    MGM Chamber Orchestra, Arthur Winograd, cond.
    MGM 3334
Quiet City
    Eastman-Rochester Orchestra, Howard Hanson, cond.
    Mercury MG-50076
Red Pony: Grandfather's Story
    Little Orchestra Soceity, Thomas Scherman, cond.
    Decca 9616
Tender Land (suite from the opera): Love Music
    Boston Symphony Orchestra, Aaron Copland, cond.
    Victor LM-2401   stereo LSC-2401

CORELLI, ARCANGELO (1653-1713)

Adagio in G Minor
    Bernard Fonteny, cello
    J. F. Paillard Chamber Orchestra
    Musical Heritage Soceity MHS 595
Church Trio Sonatas, Opus 1
    No. 1 in F Major: Mvt. III
    No. 2 in E Minor: Mvt. III
    No. 3 in A Major: Mvts. I and III
    No. 4 in A Minor: Mvt. II

CORELLI, ARCANGELO (Cont.)

No. 5 in B Flat Major: Mvt. I
No. 6 in B Minor: Mvt. I
No. 10 in G Minor: Mvt. III
No. 11 in D Minor: Mvts. I, III
Musicorum Arcadia
3 Vox DL-263

Chamber Trio Sonatas, Opus 2
No. 3 in C Major: Mvt. III
No. 4 in E Minor: Mvt. I
No. 8 in B Minor: Mvt. I
No. 9 in F Major: Mvt. II
No. 10 in E Major: Mvt. II
Musicorum Arcadia
3 Vox DL-263

Church Trio Sonatas, Opus 3
No. 1 in F Major: Mvt. I
No. 2 in D Major: Mvts. I, III
No. 3 in B Flat Major: Mvts. I, III
No. 4 in B Minor: Mvt. I
No. 5 in D Minor: Mvt. IV
No. 6 in G Major: Mvts. I, III
No. 7 in E Minor: Mvts. I, III
No. 8 in C Major: Mvts. I, III
No. 9 in F Minor: Mvts. I, III
No. 10 in A Minor: Mvt. III
No. 11 in G Minor: Mvts. I, III
Musicorum Arcadia
3 Vox DL-163

Chamber Trio Sonatas, Opus 4
No. 1 in C Major: Mvt. III
No. 2 in G Minor: Mvt. I
No. 3 in A Major: Mvts. I and III
No. 4 in D Major: Mvts. I and III
No. 5 in A Minor: Mvt. I
No. 7 in F Major: Mvt. I
No. 8 in D Minor: Mvt. I
No. 9 in B Flat Major: Mvts. I, III
No. 10 in G Major: Mvt. I
No. 11 in C Minor: Mvt. I
No. 12 in B Minor: Mvt. I
Musicorum Arcadia
3 Vox DL-163

Concerti for Strings, Opus 5
No. 1 in D Major: Mvt. III
No. 2 in B Flat Major: Mvts. I, III
No. 3 in D Major: Mvts. I, III
No. 4 in F Major: Mvts. I, IV
No. 5 in G Minor: Mvt. III
No. 6 in A Major: Mvts. I, III
No. 7 in D Minor: Mvt. III
No. 8 in E Minor: Mvts. I, III
No. 9 in A Major: Mvt. I
No. 10 in F Major: Mvts. I, III
No. 11 in E Minor: Mvt. I
Gli Accademici di Milano, Dean Eckertsen, cond.
3 Vox DL-423

Concerti Grossi for Strings, Opus 6
No. 1 in D Major: Mvt. III
No. 2 in F Major: Mvt. III

CORELLI, ARCANGELO (Cont.)

No. 3 in C Minor: Mvt. III
No. 5 in B Flat Major: Mvt. II
No. 6 in F Major: Mvt. III
No. 8 in G Minor: Mvt. V
No. 11 in B Flat Major: Mvts. III, IV
English Baroque Orchestra, Argeo Quadri, cond.
Westminster 18038/40

Concerto for Oboe and Strings: Mvts. I, III
Pierre Pierlot, oboe
Paris Philharmonic Orchestra, Rene Leibowitz, cond.
Oceanic 29

Concerto for Organ and Strings in C Major: Mvt. II
E. Power Biggs, organ
Arthur Fiedler Sinfonietta
Victor Album M-924 (78 rpm)

Fragment
The Jaye Comsort of Viols, Grayston Burgress
Turnabout TV-4017

Sonata for Organ and Strings in D Major: Mvt. III
E. Power Biggs, organ
Arthur Fiedler Sinfonietta
Victor Album M-924 (78 rpm)

Suite for String Orchestra (arr. Pinelli): Mvt. I
The Philadelphia Orchestra, Eugene Ormandy, cond.
Columbia ML-5417   stereo MS-6095

CORRETTE, MICHEL (1709-1795)

Concerto for Four Bassoons and Harpsichord: Mvt. II
Hongne, Droulez, Sennedat, Maugendre, Becksteiner
Westminster 18694

Concerto for Flute in E Minor: Aria
Klaus Pohlers, flute,
Mainze Chamber Orchestra, Günter Kehr
Turnabout TV-4010

Concerto for Three Flutes, Organ and Strings Mvt. II
Rampal, Hereche, Larde, Alain
Westminster 18694

Concerto for Harpsichord, Flute and Strings
in D Minor, Opus 26, No. 6: Mvt. II
Mainze Chamber Orchestra, Gunter Kehr
Turnabout TV-4010

COUPERIN, FRANCOIS (1668-1733)

Apotheose de Lully: Plainte des Memes (arr. Sauger)
Hewitt Chamber Orchestra, Maurice Hewitt, cond.
Epic LC-3383

Concert No. 6 in B Flat Major: Mvts. I, III
Jean-Pierre Rampal, flute
Orchestra conducted by Fernand Oubradous
Mercury MG-15007

Concert dans le Gout Theatral: Sarabande, Air tendre
Wiesbaden Collegium Musicum, Weyns, cond.
Capitol P-8111

COUPERIN, FRANCOIS (Cont.)

Concerts Royaux: No. 1 in G Major: Mvts. I, III
No. 2 in D Major: Mvts. I, III, V
No. 3 in A Major: Mvt. IV
No. 4 in E Minor: Mvts. I and V
Phillip Kaplan, flute; Samuel Mayes, cello
Erwin Bodky, harpsichord
Lyrichord LL-54
No. 7 in G Minor: Prelude, Allemande, Sarabande,
Fugette, Gavotte, Silicienne
Rampal, flute; Veyron-Lacroix, harpsichord
Dover HCR-5238

Concert Royal No. 10: Mvts. I, III
Concert Royal No. 14: Mvts. I, III
Huguette Fernandez, violin
Etienne Pasquier, cello
Laurence Boulay, harpsichord
Music Guild M-21

Concerto for Two Cellos (arr. Bazelaire): Mvts. II, III
Paul and Maude Tortelier, cellos
Supraphon LPV-474

First Concert en Sextuor: No. 1   La Livri
Toulouse Chamber Orchestra, Louis Auriacombe, cond.
Music Guild M-4

L'Espagnole (from "The Nations") (in part)
La Francoise (from "The Nations") (excerpts)
Jacobean Ensemble, Thurston Dart
Oiseau Lyre OL-50182

La Piémontoise: Air, Sarabande
Jacobean Ensemble, Thurston Dart
Oiseau Lyre OL-50182

Le Parnasse, l'Apothéose de Corelli: Mvts. I, III, IV
Claude Monteux, flute; Harry Shulman, oboe;
Bernard Greenhouse, cello; Sylvia Marlowe, harpsichord
Esoteric 517

Mass For The Parishes: Kyrie (in part)
Gloria (in part)
Benedictus
Robert Noehren, organ of the First Presbyterian Church
in Deerfield, Illinois
Lyrichord LL-128

Mass For The Converts: Kyrie (in part)
Robert Noehren, organ
Lyrichord LL-130

Messe a L'usage des Couvents: (Five Selections)
Andre Marchal, organ of the Prytanee Militaire
Westminster 18674

Pieces en Concerts: Prelude, Sicilienne, Plainte
Pierre Fournier, cello
Stuttgart Chamber Orchestra, Karl Münchinger, cond.
London LL-687

Recit de tierce en taille
Pierre Froidebise, organ of the Church of Saint-Laurent,
d'Alkmaar
Nonesuch H-1020

Sonata "La Steinkerque": Mvts. III, VI
Paris Baroque Ensemble
Music Guild M-32   stereo (S)-111

COUPERIN, FRANCOIS (Cont.)

Suite For Violes, No. 2 in E Minor: Mvt. III
Desmond Dupre, viola da gamba
Dennis Nesbitt, viola da gamba
Thurston Dart, Harpsichord
Oiseau Lyre OL-50164

COUPERIN, LOUIS (c. 1626-1661)

Chancone ne ré
Pierre Frobidebise, organ of the Church of Saint-Laurent
d'Alkmaar
Nonesuch H-1020

COWELL, HENRY (1897-   )

Ballad
Vienna Orchestral Society, F. Charles Adler, cond.
Unicorn 1045

String Quartet No. 5 (1962): Mvt. III
Beaux-Arts String Quartet
Columbia ML-5788

Symphony No. 5 (1948): Mvt. II (in part)
Vienna Symphony Orchestra, Dean Dixon, cond.
Desto D-406

Symphony No. 7 (1952): Mvt. II
Vienna Symphony Orchestra, William Strickland, cond.
Composers Recordings, Inc. CRI-142

Symphony No. 11 (1954): Mvt. I
The Louisville Orchestra, Robert Whitney, cond.
Louisville LOU-545-2

CRESTON, PAUL (1906-   )

Partita for Flute, Violin and String Orchestra: Mvts. II, IV
American Recording Society Orchestra, Walter Hendl, cond.
American Recording Society 23

Quartet for Strings, Opus 8: Andante Ecclesiastico
Hollywood String Quartet
Capitol P-8260

Symphony No. 2, Opus 35: Mvt. I (in part)
National Symphony Orchestra, Howard Mitchell, cond.
Westminster W-9708

Walt Whitman Suite, Opus 53: Mvt. IV
Academy Symphony Orchestra of Rome, Nicola Rescigno, cond.
Victor LM-2426

DAHL, INGOLF (1912-   )

The Tower of Saint Barbara: Mvt. III
The Louisville Orchestra, Robert Whitney, cond.
Louisville LOU-562

DANDRIEU, JEAN F. (1682-1738)

Premier Livre D'Orgue: Tierce en taille
Concert de Flutes
Melville Smith, Organist
Cambridge CRS-506

Recit de nazard
Jan Tomasow, violin solo
Vienna State Opera Ch. Orchestra
Vanguard SRV-154 SD

DANZI, FRANZ (1763-1826)

Quartet for Bassoon and Strings in C: Mvt. II
Arthur Grossman, bassoon; Martin Friedmann, violin
Guillermo Figueroa, viola; Ennio Orazi, cello
Lyrichord LL-154

Quintet in B Flat, Opus 56, No. 1: Mvt. II
Quintet in E Minor, Opus 67, No. 2: Mvt. II
Quintet in G Minor, Opus 56, No. 2: Mvt. II
New York Woodwind Quintet
Nonesuch H-1108 stereo 70118

Sinfonia Concertante in E Flat: Mvt. II
Vienna Radio Orchestra, Hermann Scherchen, cond.
Westminster 19100 stereo 17100

DAUVERGNE, ANTOINE (1713-1797)

Concert des Simphonies, Opus 3, No. 1: Overture; Aire
Orchestra de Chambre, Gerard Cartigny, cond.
Music Guild M-18

Third Concerto of the Four Part Symphonies,
Opus 4 in B Minor: Mvts. I, II
Jean Francois Paillard Chamber Orchestra
Musical Heritage Society 521

De ALVARADO, DIEGO (unknown - 1643)

Teinto sobre el "Pange Lingua" Espanol
Organ of the Cathedral of Segovia, Padre Jose Maria Mancha
Musical Heritage MHS-603

DEBUSSY, CLAUDE (1862-1918)

Berceuse Héröique
Amsterdam Concertgebouw, Eduard Van Beinum, cond.
Epic LC-3477

Children's Corner Suite (arr. Caplet): The Little Shepherd
Leopold Stokowski and Orchestra
Victor LM-4075

Demoiselle Élue: Prelude
The Philadelphia Orchestra, Eugene Ormandy, cond.
Columbia ML-4075

Épigraphes Antiques
Orchestre de la Suisse Romande, Ernest Ansermet, cond.
London LL-992

Martyre de Saint Sebastien: Le Cour des Lys, Le bon Pasteur
Orchestre de la Suisse Romande, Ernest Ansermet, cond.
London CM-9228

Nocturnes for Orchestra: Clouds
Orchestre de la Suisse Romande, Ernest Ansermet, cond.
London CM-9230 stereo CS-6023

Petite Suite (arr. Busser) En Bateau
NBC Symphony Orchestra, Fritz Reiner, cond.
Victor LM-1724

Prélude à l'Après-midi d'un Faune
Orchestre de la Suisse Romande, Ernest Ansermet, cond.
London CM-9228 stereo CS-6021

Quartet for Strings in G Minor, Opus 10 (1893): Mvt. III
Juilliard String Quartet
Victor LM-2413 stereo LSC-2413

Sonata for Flute, Viola and Harp: Mvt. I
Julius Baker, flute; Lillian Fuchs, viola;
Laura Newell, harp
Decca DL-9777

46

DELIUS, FREDERICK (1862-1934)

A Song Before Sunrise
> Royal Philharmonic Orchestra, Sir Malcolm Sargent, cond.
> Angel 36285

Brigg Fair, An English Rhapsody
> London Symphony Orchestra, Anthony Collins, cond.
> London CM-9066

Concerto for Cello and Orchestra (entire)
> Jacqueline Du Pre, cello
> Royal Philharmonic Orchestra, Sir Malcolm Sargent, cond.
> Angel 36285

Concerto for Violin
> Albert Sammons, violin
> Liverpool Philharmonic, Sir Malcolm Sargent, cond.
> Columbia album 672 (78 rpm)

Deux Aquarelles (arr. Fenby): No. 1
> The Halle Orchestra, Sir John Barbirolli, cond.
> His Master's Voice C-3864 (78 rpm)

Fennimore and Gerda: Intermezzo
> Royal Philharmonic Orchestra, Sir Thomas Beecham, cond.
> Capitol G-7116 stereo SG-7116

Florida Suite (edited and revised by Beecham):
> Daybreak (band 2a)
> By The River (band 3)
> Sunset (band 1a)
> At Night (band 1, side 2)
> Royal Philharmonic Orchestra, Sir Thomas Beecham, cond.
> Capitol G-7193 stereo SG-7193

Hassan, Incidental Music: Intermezzo, Interlude, Serenade
> Royal Philharmonic Orchestra, Sir Thomas Beecham, cond.
> Columbia ML-5268

In A Summer Garden
> London Symphony Orchestra, Anthony Collins, cond.
> London LL-923

Irmelin: Prelude
> Cleveland Symphony Orchestra, George Szell, cond.
> Epic LC-3330

North Country Sketches: The Wind Soughs in the Trees
> Royal Philharmonic Orchestra, Sir Thomas Beecham, cond.
> Columbia ML-4637

On Hearing The First Cuckoo In Spring
Song of Summer
> London Symphony Orchestra, Anthony Collins, cond.
> London CM 9066

Serenade from "Hassan"
> Cleveland Sinfonietta, Louis Lane, cond.
> Epic BC-1275

Summer Night On The River
> Royal Philharmonic Orchestra, Sir Thomas Beecham, cond.
> Capitol G-7116 stereo SG-7116

Walk To The Paradise Garden
> London Symphony Orchestra, Anthony Collins, cond.
> London CM-9066

DELLO JOIO, NORMAN (1913-   )

Air Power, Symphonic Suite: Lonely Pilot's Letter Home
> The Philadelphia Orchestra, Eugene Ormandy, cond.
> Columbia ML-5214 stereo MS-6029

DELLO JOIO, NORMAN (Cont.)

Meditations on Ecclesiastes: (in part)
    Oslo Philharmonic Orchestra, Alfredo Antonini, cond.
    Composers Recordings, Inc. CRI-110

DITTERSDORF, KARL DITTERS VON (1739-1799)

Concerto in E Minor for Flute: Mvt. II
    Kurt Redel, flute
    Pro Arte Chamber Orchestra of Munich
    Westminster WST-17060

Oboe Concerto in G Major: Mvt. II
    Evert Van Tricht, oboe
    Vienna Symphony Orchestra, Bernard Paumgartner, cond.
    Mercury MG-50403

Symphony in F Minor: Mvts. I, III
    Egon Parolari, oboe
    Winterthur Symphony Orchestra, Clemens Dahinden, cond.
    Record Hunter Rarities Collection RC-1227

DOHNANYI, ERNST VON (1877-1960)

Konzertstück for Cello and Orchestra, Opus 12: Mvt. II
    Janos Starker, cello
    Philharmonia Orchestra, Walter Susskind, cond.
    Angel 35627

Quartet for Strings in D Flat Major: Mvt. III
    Stradivari String Quartet
    Stradivari 614

Ruralia Hungarica: Mvts. I, III, IV
    Hungarian State Orchestra, György Lehel
    Westminster 19001

Serenade for String Trio: Andante con Variazione
    Arnold Eidus, violin; Mankovitz, viola
    George Ricci, cello
    Stradivari 614

DONIZETTI, GAETANO (1797-1877)

Concertino in G Major for English Horn: Fragment
    Lardrot, Horn
    I Solisti di Zagreb, Janigro, cond.
    Vanguard VRS-1133

Quartet for Strings in D Major: Mvt. II
    Quartetto di Roma
    His Master's Voice DB-4649 (78 rpm)

Quartet for Strings in D Minor: Mvt. II
    Quartetto della Scale
    Telefunken 66063

DONOVAN, RICHARD (1891-   )

Suite for Oboe and String Orchestra: Mvt. II
    Genovese, oboe
    Baltimore Little Symphony, Reginald Stewart, cond.
    Vanguard 468

DORATI, ANTAL (1906-   )

Nocture for Oboe and String Quartet
    Roger Lord, oboe, Allegri String Quartet
    Mercury MG-50248 stereo 90499

DOWLAND, JOHN (1562-1626)

Lachrimae Amantis Pavan
Lachrimae Antiquae Pavan
Lachrimae Antiquae Novae Pavan
Lachrimae Coactae Pavan
Lachrimae Gementes Pavan
Lachrimae Tristes Pavan
Lachrimae Verae Pavan
M. John Langton's Pavan
Captaine Digorie Piper his Galiard
M. Bucton's Galiard
M. Henry Noel his Galiard
M. Thomas Collier his Galiard
The Earl of Essex Galiard
Sir Henry Umpton's Funerall
Semper Dowland semper dolens
London Philomusia, Thurston Dart, Cond.
L'Oiseau Lyre OL-50163

DUCAURROY, EUSTACHE (1549-1609)

Five Fantasias on "Une Juene Fillette"
Pardessus de Viole, Tenor Viola da Gamba
Discant Viola da Gamba
Bass Viola da Gamba (2)
Recorder and Tenor Trombone
Concentus Musicus
Bach Guild BG-626

Fantasie No. 24
Viol Quartet, Schola Cantorum Basiliensis
Musical Heritage MHS 598

DUFF, ARTHUR (1899-1956)

Irish Suite for Strings: Nos. i and 3
Radio Eireann Symphony, Milan Horvat, cond.
Decca 9844

DUKAS, PAUL (1865-1935)

Symphony in C Major: Mvt. II
Orchestre des Concerts Colonne, Georges Sebastian, cond.
Urania 7102

DUPRÉ, MARCEL (1886-   )

"Le Chemin de la Croix: Parts 4 and 8
Marcel Dupré, organ of Saint-Sulpice
Westminster XWN 18916

DURANTE, FRANCESCO (1684-1755)

Concerto for Strings in G Minor: Mvt. III
Virtuosi de Roma, Renato Fasano, cond.
Decca 9730

Concerto No. 1 for Strings in F Minor: Mvt. II
Concerto No. 5 for Strings in A Major: Mvt. II
Scarlatti Orchestra of Napels, Thomas Schippersm, cond.
Angel 35335

Preghiera
Societa Corelli
RCS Italiana LM-20004

DUREN, GUSTAF

Allemande
Camerata Lutetiensis
Nonesuch HC-73014

49

DVORAK, ANTONIN (1841-1904)

Bagatelles for Two Violins, Cello and Harmonium
Opus 47, No. 2 Grazioso
Opus 47, No. 4 Canon. Andante con moto
Members of the Vlach Quartet
Artia ALP-706

Concerto for Cello in B Minor, Opus 104: Mvt. II
Janos Starker, cello
Philharmonic Orchestra, Walter Susskind, cond.
Angel 35417

Concerto for Violin in A Minor, Opus 53: Mvt. II
Nathan Milstein, violin
Pittsburgh Symphony William Steinberg, cond.
Capitol P-8382

Notturno for Strings, Opus 40
Boyd Neel Orchestra, Cedric Dumont, cond.
Epic LC-3350

Quartet in A Major, Opus 2 (1862): Mvt. II
Quartet in G Major, Opus 106: Mvt. II
The Kohon Quartet
Vox VBX-50 stereo SVBX-550

Quartet in A Minor, Opus 16 (1874): Mvt. II
Quartet in D Minor, Opus 34 (1877): Mvt. III
Quartet in E, Opus 80
The Kohon String Quartet
VOX VBX-49 stereo SVBX-549

Quartet for String in G Major, Opus 18: Mvt. III
Dvorak Quartet and Frantisek Posta, bass
Supraphone 10186

Quartet No. 3 for Strings in E Flat Major, Opus 51: Mvt. III
Quartet No. 6 for Strings in F Major, Opus 96: Mvt. II
Budapest String Quartet
Columbia ML-5143

Quartet No. 7 for Strings in A Flat Major: Opus 105: Mvt. III
Janacek String Quartet
Decca 9919

Quintet No. 3 in E Flat Major, Opus 97: Mvt. III
The European String Quartet
Westminster WST-17099

Romance for Violin and Orchestra, Opus 11
Joseph Suk, violin
Czech Philharmonic Orchestra, Karel Ancerl, cond.
Artis ALP-193

Serenade for Strings in E· Major, Opus 22: Mvts. III, IV
Israel Philharmonic Orchestra, Rafael Kubelik, cond.
London CM-9025 stereo STS-15037

Serenade for Strings and Winds in D Minor, Opus 44: Mvt. III
The Halle Orchestra, Sir John Barbirolli, cond.
Mercury MG-50041

Suite in A Major, Opus 89b: Mvt. IV
Czech Philharmonic Orchestra
Artia ALP-193

Suite in D Major, Opus 39 "Czech": Mvt. II
Winterthur Symphony Orchestra, Henry Swoboda, cond.
Concert Hall Society 1157

Symphony No. 1 in C Minor, Opus 3 (1865): Mvt. II
Prague Symphony Orchestra, Vaclav Neumann, cond.
Artia 140

DVORAK, ANTONIN (Cont.)

Symphony No. 2 in B Flat, Opus 4: Mvt. II
Prague Symphony Orchestra, Vaclav Neumann
Artia ALP-141

Symphony No. 3 in E Flat Major, Opus 10 (1873): Mvt. II (part one)
Prague Symphony Orchestra, Vaclav Smetacek, cond.
Artia 136   stereo S-136

Symphony No. 4 in D Minor, Opus 13 (1874): Mvt. II
Prague Symphony Orchestra, Vaclav Neumann, cond.
Artia 137   stereo S-137

Symphony No. 5 in F Major, Opus 76 (1875): Mvt. II
Czech Philharmonic Orchestra, Karel Sejna, cond.
Artia 171

Symphony No. 6 in D Major, Opus 60: Mvt. II
Czech Philharmonic Orchestra, Karel Sejna, cond.
Artia ALP-172

Symphony No. 7 in D Minor, Opus 70 (1885): Mvt. II
Berlin Philharmonic Orchestra, Ferdinand, cond.
Decca 9909

Symphony No. 8 in G Major, Opus 88: Mvts. II, III
Czech Philharmonic Orchestra, Vaclav Talich, cond.
Artia ALP-178

Twelve Cypresses: 1,2,3,4,5,6,7,9 and 10
Berkshire String Quartet
VOX VBX-51   stereo SVBX-551

Water Sprite, Opus 107: excerpts
Czech Philharmonic Orchestra, Zdenek Chalabala, cond.
Artia ALP-201

Wood Dove (in part) Opus 110
Radio Leipzig Symphony, Fritz Lehmann, cond.
Avon AV-3012

EARLS, PAUL (1934-   )

And On The Seventh Day
Eastman-Rochester Orchestra, Howard Hanson, cond.
Mercury MG-50053*   stereo 90053

EFFINGER, CECIL (1914-   )

Little Symphony No. 1 (1945): Mvts. I, III
Columbia Symphony Orchestra, Zoltan Rozsnyai, cond.
Columbia ML-5997   stereo CMS-6597

EGK, WERNER (1901-   )

French Suite after Rameau: Mvt. III
RIAS Symphony, Ferenc Fricsay, cond.
Decca 9861

Geigenmusik: Mvt. II
Leipzig Gewandhaus Orchestra, Egk, cond.
Urania 7022

EISENSTEIN, ALFRED (1899-   )

Adagio Lamentoso
Petit Suite: Lullaby
Great Vienna Broadcasting Orchestra, Varaday, cond.
Concert Classics 4151

----

*Music for Quiet Listening Album.

ELGAR, EDWARD (1857-1934)

Chanson de Nuit
London Philharmonic Orchestra, Sir Adrian Boult, cond.
London LL-1335

Concerto for Cello in E Minor: Mvt. II
Anthony Pini, cello
London Philharmonic Orchestra, Eduard van Beinum, cond.
London LPS-95

Concerto for Violin in B Minor: Mvt. II
Alfredo Campoli, violin
London Philharmonic Orchestra, Sir Adrian Boult, cond.
London LL-1168

Dream Children, Opus 43, Nos. 1 and 2
London Proms Orchestra, Raymond Agoult, cond.
Victor LM-2326   stereo LSC-2800

Dream of Gerontius, Opus 38: Prelude
London Philharmonic Orchestra, Sir Malcolm Sargent, cond.
Angel 3543-B

Elegy for Strings, Opus 58
The Halle Orchestra, Sir John Barbirolli, cond.
His Master's Voice B-9567 (78 rpm)

Nursery Suite: The Serious Doll
Liverpool Philharmonic Orchestra, Sir Malsolm Sargent, cond.
English Columbia DX-1120   (78 rpm)

Serenade for Strings in E Minor, Opus 20: Mvt. II
Boyd Neel Orchestra, Cedric Dumont, cond.
Epic LC-3350

Sospiri, Opus 70
BBC Symphony Orchestra, Sir Adrian Boult, cond.
Victor album M-635   (78 rpm)

Symphony No. 1 in A Flat Major, Opus 55: Mvt. III
London Philharmonic Orchestra, Sir Adrian Boult, cond.
His Master's Voice LHMV-1036

Wand of Youth, Suite No. 1: Fairy Pipers
                              Serenade
                              Slumber Song
                              Minuet
Wand of Youth, Suite No. 2: Fountain Dance
London Philharmonic, Eduard van Beinum, cond.
London LL-1587

ELIAS, JOSE

Ave Regina Coelorum: Preludio
New York Sinfonietta, Goberman, cond.
Musical Heritage·Society MHS V-16

ELIZALDE, FEDERICO (1907-   )

Concerto for Violin and Orchestra: Mvt. II
Christian Ferras, violin
London Symphony, Gaston Poulet, cond.
London LPS-564

ENESCO, GEORGES (1881-1955)

Symphony No. 1 in E Flat Major, Opus 13 (1906): Mvt. II
Rumanian State Symphony, George Georgescu, cond.
Artia 118

ERICH, DANIEL

Allein zu dir, Herr Jesu Christ
Jorgen Ernst Hansen, organ
Nonesuch H-1105

FALLA, MANUEL DE (1876-1946)
El Amor Brujo: The Magic Circle
  London Philharmonic, Anthony Collins, cond.
  Richmond 19032

Homages: To Paul Dukas
  Rome Symphony Orchestra, Juan Castro, cond.
  Victor LM-2143

FARRANT, DANIEL (16th—17th Century)
Four Note Pavan
  Boyd Neel String Orchestra
  Oiseau Lyre OL-50127

FASCH, JOHANN FRIEDRICH (1688-1758)
Concerto in F for Two Oboes, Two Bassons, Two Horns
and String Orchestra: Mvt. II
  The Paillard Chamber Orchestra
  Musical Heritage Society 549

Sonata in B Flat for Two Oboes da caccia and Bass: Mvt. III
  Hans Georg Renner and Dietmar Keller
  Helmut Böcher, bossoon; Fritz Neumeyer, harpsichord
  Mace M-9027

FAURE, GABRIEL (1845-1924)
Dolly, Suite (orchestrated by Rabaud): Lullaby
         Garden of Dolly
         Tenderness
  Paris Opera Orchestra, Georges Tzipine, cond.
  Angel 35311

Elegy for Cello and Orchestra, Opus 24
  Janos Starker, cello
  Philharmonia Orchestra, Walter Sussking, cond.
  Angel 35417

Masques et Bergamasques, Opus 112: Pastorale
  Hamburg Philharmonia, Arthur Winograd, cond.
  MGM 3434

Pélleas et Mélisande, Opus 80: Sicilienne
  Detroit Symphony, Paul Paray, cond.
  Mercury MG-50035

Shylock Suite, Opus 57: Epithalamium and Nocturne
  Hamburg Philharmonia, Heinz Steinecke, cond.
  MGM E-3520

String Quartet, Opus 121: Mvts. I, II
  The Loewemguth Quartet
  VOX VBX-70 XVBS-570

FERRABOSCO, ALFONSO (1543-1588)
Four Note Pavan
  Boyd Steel String Orchestra
  Oiseau Lyre OL-50127

FERRABOSCO, II (1575-1628)
Pavan
  The Jaye Comsort of Viols, Grayston Burgess
  Turnabout TV-4017

FIBICH, ZDENEK (1850-1900)
Symphony No. 3 in E Minor, Opus 53: Mvt. II
  Czech Philharmonic Orchestra, Karel Sejna, cond.
  Supraphone SUA 10396

FILTZ, ANTON (1730-1760)

Sinfonia a 8: Mvt. II
Kammerorchester des Saarländischen Rundfunks,
Karl Ristenpart, conductor
Electrola 91 103

Symphony in E Flat Major: Mvt. II
Boyd Neel String Orchestra, Neel, cond.
English Decca K-1680 (78 rpm)

FINE, IRVING (1914-   )

Serious Song, Lament for String Orchestra
The Louisville Orchestra, Robert Whitney, cond.
Louisville LOU-576

FINNEY, ROSS LEE (1906-   )

Quartet No. 6 in F Major: Mvt. III
The Stanely Quartet of the University of Michigan
Composers Recordings, Inc. CRI-116

FIOCCO, GIOSEFFO (1686-1746)

Adagio
Harry Shulman, oboe
Orchestra directed by Daniel Saidenberg
Kapp 9041   stereo S-9041

FIORENZA, NICOLA (unknown)

Concerto in D for Flute, String and Harpsichord: Mvts. I, III
Meylan, flute
Saar Chamber Orchestra, Ristenpart, cond.
Odyssey 32 16 0015   stereo 32 16 0016

Siciliana in C Minor for Strings and Harpsichord
Saar Chamber Orchestra, Ristenpart, cond.
Odyssey 32 16 0015

FISCHER, JOHANN CHRISTIAN (1733-1800)

Concerto No. 2 in E Flat for Oboe and Orchestra: Mvt. II
Andre Lardrot, oboe
Wiener Solisten, Wilfried Böttcher
Vanguard VRS-1100   stereo - 2138

FLACTON, WILLIAM (1709-1798)

Sonata in G Major: Mvt. I
Paul Doktor, viola
Marylin Mason, organ
Mirrosonic RM-1013

FOOTE, ARTHUR (1853-1937)

Night Piece for Flute and Strings (1917)
Maurice Sharp, flute
Cleveland Sinfonietta, Louis Lane, cond.
Epic LC-3754   stereo BC-1116

FOSS, LUCAS (1922-   )

Quartet No. 1 for Strings: Mvt. II
American Art Quartet
Columbia ML-5746

54

FRANCAIX, JEAN (1912-   )

L'Horloge de Flore, Suite for Oboe and Orchestra (1961):
    1. Galant de jour
    3. Cierge à grandes fleurs
    4. Ñyctanthe du Malabar
    5. Belle-de-nuit
John de Lancie, oboe
London Symphony Orchestra, André Previn, cond.
Victor LSC-2945

Quintet for Wood-winds (1948): Mvt. II
Southwest German Radio Wind Instrument Quintet
Mace M-9034

Serenade for Twelve Instruments: Mvt. II
Hamburg Chamber Orchestra, Eugen Jochum, cond.
Capitol L-8051

Symphony for Strings: Mvt. II
MGM String Orchestra, Carlos Surinach, cond.
MGM 3514

Trio for Strings in C Major: Mvt. III
Jean Pougnet, Frederick Riddle, Anthony Pini
Westminster 18515

FRANCK , CÉSAR (1822-1890)

Grande Pièce Symphonique, Opus 17: Andante
Charles Courboin, organ
Victor V-14279 (78 rpm)

Psyche: Le Sommeil de Psyche
Detroit Symphony, Paul Paray, cond.
Mercury MG-50029

Quartet for Strings in D Minor: Mvt. III
Loewenguth String Quartet
Epic LC-3227

FRANCK, MELCHOIR (c. 1579-1639)

Pavana and Galliarda
Philomusica of London, Thurston Dart, cond.
Oiseau Lyre OL-50175

FREDERICK THE GREAT (FREDERICK II) (1712-1786)

Sinfonia in D Major: Mvt. II
Berlin Philharmonic Orchestra, Hans van Benda, cond.
Electrola 91-100

FRESCOBALDI, GIROLAMO (1583-1643)

Fiori Musicali: Toccata per l'Elevazione
Guiseppe de Dona, organ
Vox 8780

Four Canzoni a due canti
Baroque Trio of Montreal
Mario Duschenes, flute
Melvin Berman, oboe
Kelsey Jones, organ
VOX VBX-65

Gagliarda (arr. Stokowski)
Leopold Stokowski and Orchestra
Victor LM-1875*

----

*Restful Good Music album.

FRESCOBALDI, GIROLAMO (Cont.)

Two Toccatas (arr. Ghedini)
 Orchestra Academy of St. Cecelia, Fernando Previtali, cond.
 London LL-1570

Toccata (arr. Leibowitz)
 Paris Philharmonic, René Leibowitz, cond.
 Counterpoint CPT-1502

FROBERGER, JOHANN JAKOB (1616-1667)

Toccata
 Gustav Leonhardt, organ
 Bach Guild 529

FUX, JOHANN JOSEPH (1660-1741)

Overture for Two Oboes, Two Violins, Viola
 Bassoon and Violene: Aria—Lentemente-Aria
 The Concentus Musicus, Nikolaus Harnondourt, cond.
 Bach Guild BG-690 stereo 70690

GABRIELI, GIOVANNI (1557-1612)

Canzona a 4
 Concentus Musicus
 Bach Guild BG-626

Canzona: La Spiritata"
 Camerata Lutetiensis
 Nonesuch HC-73014

Canzon Quarti toni a 15 (arr. Stokowski)
 Leopold Stokowski and Orchestra
 Victor LM-1721

Canzone for Double String Orchestra
 Stuttgart Chamber Orchestra, Karl Münchinger, cond.
 London CM-9144

Sonata piane forte
Sonata con tre violini
 Schola Cantorum Basiliensis, Wenzinger, cond.
 Archive ARC 3154 stereo ARC-73154

GADE, NIELS W. (1817-1890)

Echoes of Ossian, Overture (in part)
 Royal Danish Orchestra, Johan Hye-Knudsen
 Turnabout TV (3) 4085

Symphony No. 1 in C Minor, Opus 5: Mvt. III
 Royal Danish Orchestra, Johan Hye-Knudsen
 Turnabout TV (3) 4052

GALUPPI, BALDASSARE (1706-1785)

Concerti for String Orchestra: No. 1 in G Minor: Mvt. I
 No. 2 in G Major: Mvt. II
 No. 5 in E Flat Major: Mvt. I
 Milan Chamber Orchestra, Ennio Gerelli, cond.
 Telefunken 66057

Concerto a quattro in B Flat Major: Mvt. I
 I Musici
 Angel 35086

Concerto a quattro in C Minor: Mvt. I
 Virtuosi di Roma, Renato Fasano, cond.
 Decca 9730

Sonata in D Minor: Mvt. III
 Camerata Musicale
 Nonesuch H-70185

GARCIA-MORILLO, ROBERTO (1911-   )

Varations on a Five Note Theme: Theme, Canon
  Horn Club of Los Angeles
  Capitol SP-8525

GASSMAN, FLORIAN LEOPOLD (1729-1774)

Quartet No. 3 in E Minor: Mvt. I
  Vienna Concentus Musicus, Harnoncourt, cond.
  Telefunken SAWT 9475

GAULDIN, ROBERT (1931-   )

Pavane
      Eastman-Rochester Orchestra, Howard Hanson, cond.
      Mercury MG-50053*   stereo 90053*

GEISER, WALTER (1897-   )

Symphony in D Minor, Opus 44: Mvt. II
  Orchestre de la Suisse Romande, Ernest Ansermet, cond.
  London LL-1265

GEMINIANI, FRANCESCO (1687-1762)

Concerti Grossi, Opus 2 — No. 1 in C Minor: Mvts. I, III
                         No. 2 in C Minor: Mvts. I, III
Concerti Grossi, Opus 4 — No. 1 in D Major: Mvts. i, III
                         No. 2 in B Minor: Mvts. I, IV
  Renato Biffoli and Pio Giusto, violins
  Gil Accademici di Milano, Dean Eckertsen, cond.
  Vox DL-413-1 stereo STDL-500413

Concerti Grossi, Opus 3 — No. 1 in D Major: Mvt. III
                         No. 2 in G Major: Mvt. III
                         No. 3 in B Flat Major: Mvt. III
                         No. 6 in E Minor: Mvt. III
  English Baroque Orchestra, Hermann Scherchen, cond.
  Westminster 18002

Concerti Grossi, Opus 7 — No. 1: Mvts. I, III
                         No. 2 in D Minor: Mvts. I, II, III
                         No. 3 in D Major: Mvt. III
                         No. 5: Mvt. III
                         No. 6 in B Flat Major: Mvts. II, IV,V
  Felix Ayo, Walter Gallozzi, violin
  Bruno Giuranna, viola
  Enzo Altobelli, cello
  I Musici
  Epic LC 3467

The Enchanted Forest (three excerpts)
  Angelicum Orchestra of Milan, Newell Jenkins, cond.
  Nonesuch H-71115

GERSCHEFSKI, EDWIN (1909-   )

Saugatuck Suite: Mvt. III
  The Vienna Orchestra, F. Charles Adler, cond.
  Composers Recordings, Inc. CRI-115

GHEDINI, GIORGIO (1892-   )

Concerto for Two Cellos and Orchestra
  Benedetto Mazzacurati and Mario Gusella, cellos
  Scarlatti Orchestra of Naples, Ghedini, cond.
  Colosseum 1039

————————

*Music for Quiet Listening album

GHISELIN, JOHANNES (? — circa 1535)
La Alfonsina — trio of double reeds
Nonesuch H-1010

GIBBONS, ORLANDO (1583-1625)
Galliard for Violin, Bass Viol and Continuo
Neville Marriner and Peter Gibbs, violins
Desmond Dupre and Dennis Nesbitt, bass viols
Thurston Dart, Chamber organ and Harpsichord
L'Oiseau Lyre OL-50133

GILLIS, DON (1912-   )
Portrait Of A Frontier Town: Prairie Sunset
New Symphony Orchestra, Gillis, cond.
London 5008

GILSON, PAUL (1865-1942)
La Mer: Mvt. III — Le Crépuscule
Belgian National Orchestra, Louis Weemaels, cond.
London Int. 91121

GINASTERA, ALBERTO (1916-   )
Estancia, Ballet Suite: No. 2 — Wheat Dance
London Symphony Orchestra, Eugene Goossens, cond.
Everest 6013   stereo 3013

Pampeana No. 3 — A Pastoral Symphony: Mvt. I
The Louisville Orchestra, Robert Whitney, cond.
Louisville LOU-54510

Panambi, Ballet Suite: No. 1 — Moonlight On The Parana
No. 3 — Lament Of The Maidens
London Symphony Orchestra, Eugene Goossens, cond.
Everest 6003   stereo 3003

Variaciones Concertantes: parts 1, 2, 5, 6, 9, 10, 11
Minneapolis Symphony Orchestra, Antal Dorati, cond.
Mercury MG-50047

Villanico
Richard Elsasser, organ
MGM E-3585

GLANVILLE-HICKS, PEGGY (1912-   )
Concerto Romantico for Viola and Orchestra: Mvt. II
Walter Trampler, viola
MGM Chamber Orchestra, Carlos Surinach, cond.
MGM 3559

Sinfonia Pacifica: Mvt. II
Three Gymnopedies: No. 2
MGM Chamber Orchestra, Carlos Surinach, cond.
MGM 3336

GLAZOUNOV, ALEXANDER (1865-1936)
Concerto for Violin in A Minor: Mvt. II
Nathan Milstein, violin
Pittsburgh Symphony, William Steinberg, cond.
Capitol P-8382   stereo SP-8382

Five Novelettes, Opus 15: Interludium in Modo Antico
Hollywood String Quartet
Capitol P-8331

Raymonda, Ballet in Three Acts: Acts 1 and 2
Bolshoi Theatre Orchestra
Y. Svetlanov, conductor
MK 220-C

GLAZOUNOV, ALEXANDER (Cont.)

Scènes de Ballet: Pas d'Action
    Bolshoi Symphony, Alexander Gauk, cond.
    Period 596

GLIÈRE, REINHOLD (1875-1956)

Concerto for Horn and Orchestra: Mvt. II
    Valerie Polek, horn
    Bolshoi Threatre Orchestra, Glière, cond.
    Classic Editions — 6

Romance for Violin and Orchestra, Opus 3
    David Oistrakh, violin
    National Philharmonic, Kiril Kondrashin, cond.
    Colosseum — 149

GLUCK, CRISTOPH WILLIBALD (1714-1787)

Concerto for Flute in G Major: Mvt. II
    Hubert Barwahser, flute
    Vienna Symphony, Bernard Paumgartner, cond.
    Epic LC-3134

Dance Of The Blessed Spirits
    Hubert Barwahser, flute
    Vienna Symphony, Bernard Paumgartner, cond.
    Epic LC-3134

GOLDMARK, KARL (1830-1915)

Concerto for Violin in A Minor: Mvt. II
    Nathan Milstein, violin
    Philharmonia Orchestra, Harry Blech, cond.
    Capitol PAO-8414 stereo SP-8414

GORDON, GAVIN (1901-   )

The Rake's Progress (ballet suite): The Pure Girl
    Royal Opera House Orchestra, Constant Lambert, cond.
    Columbia ML-4229

GOSSEC, FRANCOIS JOSEPH (1734-1829)

Sinfonia in G Major, Opus 21, No. 2: Mvt. II
    MGM Chamber Orchestra, Carlos Surinach, cond.
    MGM E-3615

GOUNOD, CHARLES (1818-1893)

Petite Sinfonie for Wind Instruments: Mvt. II
    Northern Sinfonia Orchestra, Boris Brott, cond.
    Mace MCS 9065

GRAINGER, PERCY (1882-1961)

Walking Tune
    Philadelphia Woodwind Quintet
    Columbia ML-5984

Colonial Song
My Robin Is To The Greenwood Gone
    Eastman-Rochester "Pops", F. Fennell, cond.
    Mercury MG-50219

GRAUN, JOHANN GOTTLIEB (1703-1771)

Oboe d'Amore Concerto in D Major: Mvt. II
    Alfred Hertel, oboe d'Amore
    Austrian Tonkuenstler Orchestra, Topolski, cond.
    Musical Heritage MHS-714

GREFF, ARTUR DE (1862-1940)

Four Old Flemish Songs: No. 3 Wounded Is My Heart
Belgian Radio Orchestra, Franz Andre
Telefunken 66024

GREEN, BERNARD (1908-   )

Symphony: "Elegy": Mvt. II
Westphalia Symphony Orchestra, Bernard Green, cond.
VOX PL 14.080

Waltz Etudes for Orchestra: 1, 3, 4, 5, 6, 7, 8, 10
Westphalia Symphony Orchestra, Bernard Green, cond.
VOX PL-14.080

GREENE, MARUICE (1696-1755)

Introduction and Trumpet Tune
Flor Peters, organ
Period SPL-578

GRÉTRY, ANDRÉ M. (1741-1813)

Dances From "La Rosiere Republicaine": Nos. 2, 3
MGM Chamber Orchestra, Carlos Surinach, cond.
MGM-3615

Zemire et Azor: Air de ballet
London Philharmonic, Sir Thomas Beecham, cond.
Columbia Album X-215 (78rpm)

GRIEG, EDVARD (1843-1907)

Holberg Suite, Opus 40: Sarabande, Air
Stuttgart Chamber Orchestra, Karl Munchinger, cond.
London CM-9195 stereo CS-6088

Lyric Pieces: At The Cradle
MGM String Orchestra, Arthur Winograd, cond.
MGM 3221

Lyric Pieces: Secret
The Halle Orchestra, Sir John Barbirolli, cond.
His Master's Voice DB-21594 (78rpm)

Lyric Suite, Opus 54: Nocturne
Danish State Radio Orchestra, Erik Tuxen, cond.
Richmond 19053.

Norwegian Melodies, Opus 63: Cowkeeper's Tune
Two Elegiac Melodies, Opus 34: Heart Wounds, The Last Spring
London Proms Orchestra, Charles Mackerras, cond.
Victor LM-2336

Old Norwegian Romance with Variations: (in part)
Royal Philharmonic Orchestra, Sir Thomas Beecham, cond.
Angel 35339

Quartet for String in G Major, Opus 27: Mvt. II
Quilet String Quartet
MGM E-3133

Two Melodies after Original Songs, Opus 53: The First Meeting
MGM String Orchestra, Arthur Winograd, cond.
MGM 3221

GRIFFES, CHARLES, TOMLINSON (1884-1920)
Clouds
The White Peacock
   Eastman-Rochester Orchestra, Howard Hanson, cond.
   Mercury MG-50085
Poem for Flute and Orchestra (1918)
   Maurice Sharp, flute
   Cleveland Sinfonietta, Louis Lane, cond.
   Epic BC-1116

GRIGNY, NICHOLAS DE (1671-1703)
La Livre d'orgue — Bands 1.2.3.5
   Melville Smith, organist
   Cambridge CRS-506
Mass: récit de tierce en taille
Pange Lingua (Parts 2 and 3)
   Rene Saorgin, organ
   Turnabout TV 4054

GUAMI, GIOSEFFO (c. 1540-1611)
Canzone a 8
   Concentus Musicus
   Bach Guild BG-626

GUARNIERI, CAMARGO (1907-   )
Quartet No. 2 for Strings: Mvt. II
   Pascal String Quartet
   Angel 35228

GUILAIN-FREINSBERG
Cromorne dé las Suite du IVeme ton
Tierce en taille, Trio do flutes from Suite du Premiere Ton
   Michele Chapuis, organ. Organ Francois Henri Cliquot (1791)
   Cathedrale de Poitiers
   Musica Sacra AMS 30

GUYLA, DAVID (1913-   )
Concerto for Viola and Orchestra: Mvt. II
   Pál Lukács, viola
   Staatliches Konzert Orchestra, János Ferencsik, cond.
   DGG LPM-18874

HADLEY, HENRY (1871-1937)
October Twilight
   Symphony Orchestra, James, cond.
   Victor album M-634 (78 rpm)

HAHN, REYNALDO (1876-1947)
Concerto Provencale: Mvt. II
   Chamber Orchestra, Fernand Oubradous, cond.
   French HMV DA-4993/5 (78 rpm)

HAINES, EDMUND (1914-   )
Quartet No. 4 (1957): Theme and Soliloguy
   Oxford String Quartet of Miami University
   Composers Recordings, Inc. CRI 188

HANDEL, GEORGE FREDERICK (1685-1759)
Alcina Suite: Entrance of the Agreeable Dreams
   Boyd Neel Orchestra, Boyd Neel. cond.
   Unicorn 1038

HANDEL, GEORGE FREDERICK (Cont.)

Concerto a quatre No. 1 in D Minor: Mvts. i, III
 Claude Monteux, flute; Harry Shulman, oboe
 George Ricci, cello; Robert Conant, harpsichord
 American Society AS-1004 stereo S-1004

Concerti Grossi, Opus 3: No. 1 in B Flat Major: Mvt. II
　　　　　　　　　　　　No. 3 in G Major: Mvt. III
　　　　　　　　　　　　No. 5 in D Minor: Mvt. III
 Boyd Neel Orchestra, Boyd Neel. cond.
 London CM-9117

Concerti Grossi, Opus 3: No. 2 in B Flat Major: Mvt. II
　　　　　　　　　　　　No. 4 in F Major: Mvt. II
 Orchestra of the Cento Soli, Anthony Bernard, cond.
 Robert Casier, oboe soloist
 Nonesuch H-1013 stereo 71013

Concerti Grossi, Opus 6: No. 1 in G Major: Mvt. III
　　　　　　　　　　　　No. 4 in A Minor: Mvt. III
　　　　　　　　　　　　No. 5 in D Major: Mvt. III
　　　　　　　　　　　　No. 7 in B Flat Major: Mvt. II
　　　　　　　　　　　　No. 8 in C Minor: Mvts. II, IV, V
　　　　　　　　　　　　No. 10 in D Minor: Mvt. III
　　　　　　　　　　　　No. 12 in B Minor: Mvt. IV
 Boyd Neel Orchestra, Boyd Neel, Cond.
 3 London A-4311

Concerto No. 1 for Oboe in B Flat Major: Mvt. III
 Harry Shulman, oboe
 Orchestra directed by Daniel Saidenberg
 Kapp 9041 stereo 9041-S

Concerto No. 2 for Oboe in B Flat Major: Overture to Berenice
 Roger Lord, oboe
 Academy of St. Martin-In-The-Fields, Neville Marriner, cond.
 London Argo ZRG 5442

Concerto No. 3 for Oboe in G Minor: Mvt. III
 Marcel Tabuteau, oboe
 The Philadelphia Orchestra, Eugene Ormandy, cond.
 Columbia ML 4629

Concerto in C Major, "Alexanderfest": Mvt. II
 Vienna State Opera Orchestra, Felix Prohaska, cond.
 Bach Guild 506

Concerto in B Minor for Viola: Mvt. II
Concerto in G Minor for Viola: Mvts. I, III
 Vardi, viola
 Stradivari Chamber Orchestra
 Stradivari 749

Concerto in F Major for Strings and Winds: Mvt: III
 Copenhagen Collegium Musicum
 Lavard Friisholm, conductor
 Haydn Society HS-9022

Concerto in F Major for Recorder and Strings: Mvts. I, III
 The London Strings, Neville Marriner, cond.
 Mercury MG-50443

The Messiah: Pastoral Symphony
 Royal Philharmonic Orchestra, Sir Thomas Beecham, cond.
 Victor LCT-1130

Rodrigo Suite: Minuet I and II
 Philomusica of London, Anthony Lewis, cond.
 Oiseau Lyre 50170 stereo 60001

HANDEL, GEORGE FREDERICK (Cont.)

Royal Fireworks Music: Alla siciliana
>Royal Philharmonic Orchestra, Sir Malcolm Sargent, cond.
>Capitol G-7202   stereo SG-7202

Sonata for Oboe in C Minor: Mvts. I, III
Sonata for Oboe in G Minor: Mvts. I, III
>Wölsing, oboe; Medici, cello Woldike, harpsichord
>English Columbia DX-7 and DX 10   (78 rpm)

Sonatas for Violin and Figured Bass No. 1 in A Major: Mvt. III
>>No. 2 in G Minor: Mvt. III
>>No. 3 in F Major: Mvt. III
>>No. 4 in D Major: Mvt. III
>>No. 5 in D Major: Mvt. III
>>No. 6 in E Major: Mvt. III

>Alexander Schneider, violin
>Frank Miller, cello; Ralph Kirkpatrick, harpsichord
>Columbia ML-2149/51

Trio Sonata Opus 5, No. 3: Mvt. II
>Sinfonia di Roma, Domenico Savino, cond.
>Kapp 9044   stereo S-9044

Trio Sonata Opus 5, No. 6: Mvts. I, III
>Scheiderhan, Swoboda, violins
>Benesch, cello; Holetschek, harpsichord
>Westminster 18585

Trio Sonata in A Major, Opus 5, No. 1: Mvts. I, II
Trio Sonata in F Major, Opus 2, No. 4: Mvts. I, II
Trio Sonata in G Major, Opus 2, No. 5: Mvts. I, II
Trio Sonatain G Minor: Mvts. I, II
>Maxence Larrieu Instrumental Ensemble
>Musical Heritage MHS-656

HANDEL-BEECHAM

Faithful Shepherd Suite: Adagio
>London Philharmonic Orchestra, Sir Thomas Beecham, cond.
>Columbia ML-4374

Love in Bath (ballet suite): No. 5 — Love Scene
>>No. 9 — The Weary Flunkies
>>No. 10 — The Exquisites
>>No. 13 — Sarabande
>>No. 14 — Minuet
>>No. 16 — Rondeau
>>No. 19 — Interlude

>Royal Philharmonic Orchestra, Sir Thomas Beecham, cond.
>Angel 35504   stereo S-35504

Origin of Design (ballet suite): Musette
>London Philharmonic Orchestra, Sir Thomas Beecham, cond.
>Columbia 68156   (78 rpm)

HANDEL-HARTY

Water Music Suite: Mvt. II
>London Philharmonic Orchestra, Eduard van Beinum, cond.
>London CM-9067

HANDOSHKIN, IVAN (c.1740-1804)

Concerto for Viola in C Minor: Mvt. II
>Rudolf Barshai, viola
>Moscow Chamber Orchestra
>Monitor 2018

HANFF, JOHANN NICOLAUS (1630-1706)

Chorale Prelude — Ach Gott, vom Himmel seih darein
Frits Heitmann, organ
Telefunken 66037

Chorale Prelude: War Gott nicht mit uns
Flor Peeters, organ of St. Michael's Zwolle
Ogden CLP 1442

HANSON, HOWARD (1896-)

Mosaics
Eastman-Rochester Orchestra, Howard Hanson, cond.
Mercury 90430

Serenade for Flute, Harp and Strings
Eastman-Rochester Orchestra, Howard Hanson, cond.
Mercury MG-60076

HANUS, JAN (1915-)

Concertante Symphony (for organ, harp, timpani and
strings), Opus 31: Mvt. II
Czech Philharmonic Orchestra, Karel Ancerl, cond.
Supraphon SUA 10046

HARRIS, ROY (1898-

Kentucky Spring
The Louisville Orchestra, Robert Whitney, cond.
Louisville LOU-602

HARRISON, LOU (1917-)

Suite No. 2 for String Quartet: Mvt. I
New Music String Quartet
Columbia ML-4491

HARTY, HAMILTON (1879-1941)

A John Field Suite: Nocturne
Liverpool Philharmonic Orchestra
Sir Malcolm Sargent, cond.
Entre RL-3043

HASSE, JOHANN ADOLPH (1699-1783)

Concerto in A Major for Flute: Mvt. II
Schaeffer, flute
N. German Chamber Orchestra, Lange, cond.
Archive ARC-73240

Concerto in D Major for Flute: Mvt. II
Riessberger, flute
Austrian Tonkünstler Orchestra, Maerzendorfer, cond.
Musical Heritage MHS 635

Sonata for Flute and Organ in D Major: Mvt. I
Kuttruff, Vollenweider
Swiss HMV JK-10 (78 rpm)

HASSLER, HANS LEO (1564-1612)

Four Intradas
Philomusica of London, Thurston Dart, cond.
Oiseau Lyre OL-50175

HAYDN, FRANZ JOSEF (1732-1809)

Cassation in C Major for Cello — Five Mvts.
The Biodermeier Orchestra
Dr. Kurt List, conductor
Musical Heritage 544

HAYDN, FRANZ JOSEF (Cont.)

Cassation in G Major: Mvt. II
   Dresden Chamber Soloists, Marcel Bernard, cond.
   Baroque BU-1820

Concerto in C Major for Cello: Mvt. II
   Milos Sadlo, cello
   Prague Radio Symphony, Alois Klima, cond.
   Artia ALP-206

Concerto in D Major for Cello, Opus 101: Mvt. II
   Antonio Janigro, cello
   Vienna State Opera Orchestra, Felix Prohaska, cond.
   Westminster 18406

Concerto for Flute in D Major: Mvt. II
   Camillo Wanausek, flute
   Vienna Pro Musica Orchestra, F. Charles Adler, cond.
   Vox PL-10150

Concerto, in C Major for Flute, Oboe and Orchestra: Mvt. II
Concerto in F Major for Flute, Oboe and Orchestra: Mvt. II
   Rampal, flute; Pierlot, oboe
   Collegium Musicum of Paris, Roland Douatte, cond.
   Nonesuch H-1067

Concerto for Oboe in C Major: Mvt. II
   Evelyn Rothwell, oboe
   The Halle Orchestra, Sir John Barbirolli, cond.
   Mercury MG-50041

Concerto for Violin in A Major: Mvt. II
   Robert Gerle, violin
   Vienna Radio Orchestra, Robert Zeller, cond.
   Westminster WST 17016

Concerto for Violin in C Major: Mvt. II
   Szymon Goldberg, violin
   Philharmonia Orchestra, Walter Süsskind, cond.
   Decca DL-8504

Divertimento for Baryton Trio, No. 64: Mvt. I
   Salzburger Baryton Trio
   Nonesuch H-71049

Divertimenti for Baryton, Viola and Cello
         No. 37 in G Major: Mvt. II
         No. 44 in D Major: Mvt. II
         No. 109 in C Major: Mvt. II
   Salzburger Baryton Trio
   Decca Archive 3120

Divertimento in C Major: Mvt. II
   London Baroque Ensemble, Karl Haas, cond.
   Westminster 18058

Divertimento in A Major, Opus 31, No. 2: Mvt. I
Divertimento in G Major, Opus 31, No. 3: Mvt. I
Divertimento in E Flat Major a Six Stromenti: Mvt. IV
   London Baroque Ensemble, Karl Haas, cond.
   Westminster 18612 — 9055

Divertimento in F Major (Hob 11:15): Mvt. III
Divertimento in C Major (Hob. 11:14): Mvt. III
Divertimento in F Major (Hob. 11:23): Mvt. III
Divertimento in C Major (Hob. 11:7): Mvt. II
Divertimento in G Major: Mvt. III
   The Wind Ensemble of the Vienna
         State Opera Orchestra, directed
         by Wilhelm Sommer
   Amadeo AVRS-6208

HAYDN, FRANZ JOSEF (Cont.)

Divertimento for Cello and Orchestra: Mvt. I
　　Gregor Piatigorsky, cello
　　Chamber Orchestra
　　Victor LCS-2770

Divertimento terzo a otto voci: Mvt. I
　　Concentus Musicus, Wein, cond.
　　Telefunken SAWT 9475

Notturno No. 1 in C Major: Mvt. II
Notturno No. 2 in F Major: Mvt. II
　　Vienna Chamber Orchestra, Franz Litschauer, cond.
　　Haydn Society 1023

Notturno No. 6 in G Major: Mvt. II
　　Saar Chamber Orchestra, Karl Ristenpart, cond.
　　Music Guild M-35

Overture to "l'Infedelta Deluda:" Poco adagio
　　Vienna Chamber Orchestra. Carlo Zwcchi
　　Musical Heritage MHS 639

Quartets for Strings

Opus 1, No. 3 in D Major: Mvt. I
　　Schneider String Quartet
　　Haydn Society Q-2

Opus 2, No. 2, in E Major: Mvt. III
Opus 2, No. 4, in F Major: Mvt. III
　　Schneider String Quartet
　　Haydn Society Q-4/5

Opus 2, No. 5, in D Major: Mvt. III
　　Schneider String Quartet
　　Haydn Society HS-9080

Opus 3, No. 5 in F Major: Mvt. II
　　Amadeus String Quartet
　　Westminster 18609

Opus 17, No. 1, in E Major: Mvt. III
Opus 17, No. 3, in E Flat Major: Mvt. III
Opus 17, No. 4, in C Minor: Mvt. III
　　Schneider String Quartet
　　Haydn Society Q 13/14

Opus 17, No. 5, in G Major: Mvt. III
Opus 17, No. 6, in G Major: Mvt. III
　　Schneider String Quartet
　　Haydn Society HS-9085

Opus 20, No. 1, in E Flat Major: Mvt. III
　　Schneider String Quartet
　　Haydn Society Q-16

Opus 20, No. 3, in G Minor: Mvt. III
Opus 20, No. 4 in D Major: Mvt. II
Opus 20, No. 6, in A Major: Mvt. II
　　Schneider String Quartet
　　Haydn Society HS-9087/9088

Opus 33, No. 3, in C Major: Mvt. III
Opus 33, No. 4, in B Flat Major: Mvt. II
Opus 33, No. 5, in G Major: Mvt. II
Opus 33, No. 6, in D Major: Mvt. III
　　Schneider String Quartet
　　Haydn Society HS-9021

Opus 42, in D Minor: Mvt. III
　　Schneider String Quartet
　　Haydn Society Q-37

HAYDN, FRANZ JOSEF (Cont.)

Opus 50, No. 1, in B Flat Major: Mvt. II
Opus 50, No. 2, in C Major: Mvt. II
Opus 50, No. 3, in E Flat Major: Mvt. II
Opus 50, No. 4, in F Sharp Minor:
  Schneider String Quartet
  Haydn Society HS-9089/9090
Opus 50, No. 6, in D Major: Mvt. II
  Schneider String Quartet
  Haydn Society HS-9015

Opus 54, No. 1, in G Major: Mvt. II
Opus 54, No. 2, in C Major: Mvt. II
Opus 54, No. 3, in E Major: Mvt. II
  Allegri String Quartet
  Westminster XWN 19094   stereo 17094

Opus 55, No. 1, in A Major: Mvt. II
Opus 55, No. 2, in F Minor: Mvt. I
Opus 55, No. 3, in B Flat Major: Mvt. II
  Allegri String Quartet
  Westminster 19084   stereo 17084

Opus 64, No. 2, in B Minor: Mvt. II
Opus 64, No. 3, in B Flat Major: Mvt. II
Opus 64, No. 4, in G Major: Mvt. III
Opus 64, No. 5, in D Major: Mvt. II
Opus 64, No. 6, in E Flat Major: Mvt. II
  Vienna Konzerthaus Quartet
  Westminster 18603/18604/18605

Opus 71, No. 1, in B Flat Major: Mvt. II
Opus 71, No. 2, in D Major: Mvt. II
  Griller String Quartet
  Vanguard VRS-1042   stereo 2034

Opus 74, No. 2, in F Major: Mvt. II
Opus 74, No. 3, in G Major: Mvt. II
  Griller String Quartet
  Vanguard VRS-1041   stereo 2034

Opus 76, No. 1, in G Major: Mvt. II
  Budapest String Quartet
  Columbia ML-4922

Opus 76, No. 2, in D Minor: Mvt. II
  Schneider String Quartet
  Haydn Society HS-9015

Opus 76, No. 4, in B Flat Major: Mvt. II
  Budapest String Quartet
  Columbia ML-4923

Opus 76, No. 5, in D Major: Mvt. II
  Vienna Konzerthaus Quartet
  Westminster 18608

Opus 76, No. 6, in E Flat Major: Mvt. II
  Budapest String Quartet
  Columbia ML-4924

Opus 77, No. 1 in G Major: Mvt. II
  Juilliard String Quartet
  Victor LM-2168

Quartet for Flute, Opus 5, No. 1: Mvt. II
  Europa Quartet, Wanausek, flute
  Turnabout TV-4007

Scherzando in F Major: Mvt. III
  London Baroque Ensemble, Karl Hass, cond.
  Westminster 18612

HAYDN, FRANZ JOSEF (Cont.)

Sinfonia Concertante in B Flat Major, Opus 84: Mvt. II
    The Philadelphia Orchestra, Eugene Ormandy, cond.
    Columbia ML-5374   stereo MS-6061

Symphony No. 6 in D Major ("Le Matin"): Mvt. II
Symphony No. 7 in C Major ("Le Midi"): Mvt. II
Symphony No. 8 in G Major ("Le Soir"): Mvt. II
Symphony No. 12 in E Major: Mvt. II
Symphony No. 21 in A Major: Mvt. I
Symphony No. 23 in G Major: Mvt. II
Symphony No. 24 in D Major: Mvt. II
Symphony 51 in B Flat Major: Mvt. II
Symphony No. 56 in C Major: Mvt. II
    Vienna State Opera Orchestra, (late) Max Goberman, cond.
    Library of Recorded Masterpieces Subscription Set
    HS-2/3/5/7/9

Symphony No. 13 in D Major: Mvt. II
    Vienna Symphony Orchestra, Jonathan Sternberg, cond.
    Haydn Society 1001

Symphony No. 17 in F Major: Mvt. II
    Kammerorchester der Wiener Festspiele, Boettcher, cond.
    Turnabout TV-(3) 4092

Symphony No. 19 in D Major: Mvt. II
    The Little Orchestra of London, Leslie Jones, cond.
    Nonesuch H-1031   stereo 71031

Symphony No. 22 in E Flat Major: Mvt. I
    Vienna Radio Orchestra, Laszlo Somogyi, cond.
    Westminster XWN-19095   stereo 17095

Symphony No. 31 in D Major ("Hornsignal"): Mvts. II, IV
    The Little Orchestra of London, Leslie Jones, cond.
    Nonesuch H-1031   stereo 71031

Symphony No. 33 in C Major: Mvt. II
    Hamburg Philharmonia, Arthur Winograd, cond.
    MGM E-3436

Symphony No. 34 in D Minor: Mvt. I
    Vienna Symphony Orchestra, Jonothan Sternberg, cond.
    Haydn Society 1026

Symphony No. 42 in D Major: Mvt. II
    Vienna Chamber Orchestra, Franz Litschauer, cond.
    Haydn Society 1026

Symphony No. 43 in E Flat Major ("Mercury"): Mvt. II
    Danish State Radio Orchestra, Mogens Wöldike, cond.
    Haydn Society HS-9071

Symphony No. 44 in E Minor ("Trauer"): Mvt. II
    Netherlands Chamber Orchestra, Szymon Goldberg, cond.
    Epic LC-3625

Symphony No. 45 in F Sharp Minor ("Farewell"): Mvt. II
    The Little Orchestra of London, Leslie Jones, cond.
    Nonesuch H-1031   stereo 71031

Symphony No. 46 in B Major: Mvt. II
    Hamburg Philharmonia, Arthur Winograd
    MGM E-3436

Symphony No. 48 in C Major ("Maria Theresia"): Mvt. II
    Symphony Orchestra of Radio Zagreb, Janigro, cond.
    Vanguard VRS-1108   stereo 2145

Symphony No. 49 in F Minor '((La Passione"): Mvt. I
    Vienna State Opera Orchestra, Hermann Scherchen, cond.
    Westminster 18613

HAYDN, FRANZ JOSEF (Cont.)

Symphony No. 49 in F Minor ("La Passione"): Mvt. III
    The Little Orchestra of London, Leslie Jones, cond.
    Nonesuch H-1032   stereo 71032

Symphony No. 50 in C Major: Mvt. II
    Danish State Radio Orchestra, Mogens Wöldike, cond.
    Haydn Society HS-9071

Symphony No. 54 in G Major: Mvt. II
    Vienna State Academy of Music, Hans Swarowsky, cond.
    Lyrichord LL-32

Symphony No. 55 in E Flat Major ("Schoolmaster"): Mvt. II
    Vienna Symphony Orchestra, Hermann Scherchen, cond.
    Westminster 18614

Symphony No. 59 in A Major ("Fire"): Mvt. II
    Festival Chamber Orchestra, Dorati, cond.
    Mercury MG-50436   stereo 90436

Symphony No. 64 in A Major: Mvt. II
    Vienna Symphony Orchestra, Henry Swoboda, cond.
    Westminster 18615

Symphony No. 81 in G Major: Mvt. II
    Festival Chamber Orchestra, Dorati, cond.
    Mercury MG 50436   stereo 90436

Symphony No. 87 in A Major: Mvt. II
    Orchestre de la Suisse Romande, Ansermet, cond.
    London CMA-7306   stereo 2306

Trio for Flute and Strings, Opus 38, No. 5: Mvt. I
    Poul Birkelund, flute; Arne Karecki, violin;
    Alf Petersen, cello
    Vanguard 1008

Trio for Violin, Viola and Cello, Opus 53, No. 3: Mvt. I
    Pougnet, Riddle, Pini
    Westminster XWN 18609   stereo 9033

HAYDN, MICHAEL (1737-1806)

Concerto in C Major for Viola and Harpsichord: Mvt. II
    Ernst Wallfisch, viola; Lory Wallfisch, harpsichord
    Württemberg Chamber Orchestra, Jorg Faerber, cond.
    Turnabout TV (3)-4079

Quartet in D Major: Mvt. III
    Mozarteum-Quartett Salzburg
    Musical Heritage MHS-662

Quintet for Strings in G Major: Mvt. II
    The Roth String Quartet
    SFM M-1005

Symphony in D Major: Mvt. II
    Vienna Chamber Orchestra, Carlo Zwcchi
    Musical Heritage MHS 639

HELLENDAAL, PIETER (1718-1799)

Grand Concerto, Opus 3, No. 2 in D Minor: Mvts. I, II
    Amsterdam Chamber Orchestra, André Rieu, cond.
    Telefunken SAWT-9440

HELPS, ROBERT (1928-   )

Symphony No. 1 (1955): Mvt. I
    Columbia Symphony Orchestra, Rozsnyai, cond.
    Columbia ML-6201   stereo MS-6801

HEMING, MICHAEL (1920-1942)

Threnody for a Soldier Killed in Action (arr. Collins)
The Halle Orchestra, Sir John Barbirolli, cond.
His Master's Voice C-3427 (78rpm)

HENKEMANS, HANS (1913-   )

Concerto for Violin and Orchestra: Mvt. III
Theo Olof, violin
Amsterdam Concertgebouw, Eduard Van Beinum, cond.
Epic LC-3093

HENRY VIII (1491-1547)

Consort V (alto, tenor, bass recorders)
Martha Bixler, Eric Leber, Morris Newmann
Trio Flauto Dolce 1

HENZE, HANS WERNER (1926-   )

Symphony No. 1 (1947): Mvt. II
Berlin Philharmonic, Henze, cond.
DDG 139203

Symphony No. 5 (1962): Mvt. II
Berlin Philharmonic, Henze, cond.
DDG 139203

Concerto in E Minor for Cello, Opus 30: Mvt. II
George Miquelle, cello
Eastman-Rochester Orchestra, Howard Hanson, cond.
Mercury MG-50163   stereo 90163

HINDEMITH, PAUL (1895-   )

Concerto for Cello (1940): Mvt. II (in part)
Paul Tortelier, cello
Czech Philharmonid Orchestra, Karel Ancerl, cond.
Supraphon LPV-474

Concerto for Clarinet and Orchestra (1947): Mvt. III
Louis Cahuzac, clarinet
Philharmonia Orchestra, Paul Hindemith, cond.
Angel 35490

Concerto for Violin and Orchestra (1940): Mvt. II (in part)
Joseph Fuchs, violin
London Symphony, Eugene Goossens, cond.
Everest 6040   stereo 3040

Concerto for Violin, Opus 36, No. 3: Nachstuck
Robert Gerle, violin
Chamber Orchestra, Hermann Scherchen , cond.
Westminster WST-17087

Five Pieces for String Orchestra, Opus 44, No. 4: Mvts. I and IV
Stuttgart Chamber Orchestra, Karl Munchinger, cond.
London LL-1395

Five Pieces for String Orchestra, Opus 44, No. 4: Mvt. I
Maurice Levine String Orchestra, Maurice Levine, cond.
MGM E-3161

Herodiade (excerpts)
The MGM Orchestra, Arthur Winograd, cond.
MGM E-3683

Kammermusik, Opus 24, No. 1: Mvt. II
San Francisco Little Symphony, Gregory Millar, cond.
Fantasy 5001

Kleine Kammermusik, Opus 24, No. 2: Mvt. III
Wind Quintet of the French National Radio Orchestra
Angel 35079

70

HINDEMITH, PAUL (Cont.)

Nobilissima Visione (ballet suite) (1938): Introduction and
rondo Pastorale
Philharmonia Orchestra, Paul Hindemith, cond.
Angel 35490

Octet (1958): Mvt. III
Members of the New York Woodwind Quintet and the
Fine Arts Quartet
Concert Disc 1218   stereo 218

Quartet No. 3 for Strings, Opus 22: Mvt. III
Hollywood String Quartet
Capitol P-8151

Sonata for Organ: No. 1: Mvts. II, IV
No. 2: Mvt. II
No. 3: Mvt. II
Robert Noehren, organ of Grace Episcopal Church,
Sandusky, Ohio
Lyrichord 53

Sonata for Four Horns: Fugato, Variations (in part)
Chicago Symphony Horn Quartet
Concert Disc M-1243   stereo 243

Symphonia Serena   (1947):
Philharmonia Orchestra, Paul Hindemith, cond.
Angel 35491

Trio for Strings, Opus 34, No. 1: Mvt. II
Jean Pougnet, violin; Frederick Riddle, viola
Anthony Pini, cello
Westminster 18593

HOLBORNE, ANTONY (? - 1602)

Pavan: Paradizo
Galliard: The Sighs
Pavan
The Marie-Gold
Viols: Schola Cantorum Basiliensis
Recorders: The Dolmetch Consort
Nonesuch H-3010

Pavan: "The Funerals"
Pardessus de Viole, Discant Viola da Gamba
Tenor Viola da Gamba, Bass Gambas (2)
Concentus Musicus
Bach Guild BG-626

Pavan: "The Funerals"
Boyd Neel String Orchestra, Boyd Neel, cond.
Oiseau Lyre OL-50127

HOLMBOE, VAGN (1909-   )

Quartet No. 2 for Strings, Opus 47: Mvt. IV
Musica Vitalis Quartet
London LL-1087

Quartet No. 3 for Strings, Opus 48: Mvt. V
Koppel String Quartet
London LL-1119

HOLST, GUSTAV (1874-1934)

Egdon Heath, Opus 47 (1928)
London Philharmonic Orchestra, Sir Adrian Boult, cond.
London CS-6324

HOLST,GUSTAV (Cont.)

The Planets, Opus 32 (1914-16) "Venus," "Saturn"
London Symphony Orchestra, Sir Malcolm Sargent, cond.
London CM-9101

The Perfect Fool (Ballet Music - 1921): Mvt. II
London Philharmonic Orchestra, Sir Adrian Boult , cond.
London CM-9324 stereo CS-6324

HOLZBAUER, IGNAZ (1711-1783)

Symphony in E Flat, Opus 4, No. 3: Mvt. II
Northern Sinfonia Orchestra, Boris Brott, cond.
Mace MCS-9069

Sinfonia in G Major: Mvt. II
Spielgemeinschaft der ARCHIVE Production
Wolfgang Hofmann, cond.
Archive 3159

HONEGGER, ARTHUR (1892-1955)

Concerto de Camera, Flute, English Horn, Strings (1949): Mvt. II
Cleveland Sinfonietta, Louis Lane, cond.
Epic LC-3754 stereo BC-1116

Pastorale d'ete
Concert Arts Orchestra, Valdimir Golschmann, cond.
Capitol P-8244

Sonatine for Two Violins Unaccompanied (1920): Andantino
David and Igor Oistrakh
Monitor MC-2058

HOTTETERRE, JACQUES (LOUIS) (? - c. 1760)

Sonata in B Minor for Two Flutes: Mvt. III
Helmut Riessberger, Gernot Kury, flutes
Musical Heritage MHS-574

Sonata in D Major: Grave
Michel Piquet, baroque oboe
The New York String Trio
Dover HCR-7007

HOVHANESS, ALAN (1911-   )

Alleluia and Fugue for String Orchestra: Alleluia
MGM String Orchestra, Carlos Surinach, cond.
MGM-3504

Concerto No. 1 for Orchestra, "Arevakal": Mvt. I
Eastman-Rochester Orchestra, Howard Hanson, cond.
Mercury MG-50078

Meditation on Orpheus (excerpts)
Japan Philharmonic Orchestra, William Strickland, cond.
Composers Recordings, Inc. CRI-142 stereo CRI 134

Mysterious Mountain: Mvts. I, II, III (in part)
Chicago Symphony Orchestra, Fritz Reiner, cond.
Victor LM-2251 stereo LSC-2251

Saint Vartan Symphony, Opus 80: sections 3, 4, 5, 13, 17, 20
MGM Chamber Orchestra, Carlos Surinach, cond.
MGM 3453

Symphony No. 4, Opus 165 (3 Mvts. in part)
Eastman Wind Ensemble, Clyde Roller, cond.
Mercury MG-50366 stereo 90366

Talin: Mvts. I, II
Emanuel Vardi, viola
MGM String Orchestra, Izler Solomon
MGM E-3432

HOVHANESS, ALAN (Cont.)

Tower Music for Brass and Winds, Opus 129
MGM Orchestra, Carlos Surninach, cond.
MGM 3504

HOWE, MARY (1882-1964)

Spring Pastoral (1936)
Imperial Philharmonic of Tokyo, William Strickland, cond.
Composers Recordings, Inc. CRI-145

Stars (1937)
Vienna Orchestra, William Strickland, cond.
Composers Recordings, Inc. CRI-103

HUMMEL, JOHANN NEPOMUK (1778-1837)

Quartet for Clarinet in E Flat: Mvt. III
David Glazer, clarinet
TKe Kohon Quartet
VOX DL-960

HUMPERDINCK, ENGELBERT (1854-1921)

Moorish Rhapsody: "Tarifa" (Elegy at Sunset)
Leipzig Gewandhaus, Herman Abendroth, cond.
Avon AVS-13017

IBERT, JACQUES (1890-1962)

Amours de Jupiter: in part
Paris Opera Orchestra, Ibert, cond.
Capitol P-18004

Concerto for Flute and Orchestra: Mvt. II
Graf, Winterhur Symphony, Victor Desarzens, cond.
Concert Hall Society 1109

Symphonie Concertante, Oboe and Strings (1949) Mvt. II
John De Lancie, oboe
London Symphony Orchestra, Andre Previn, cond.
Victor LM-2945

Trio for Violin, Cello and Harp: Mvt. II
Laura Newell, Stuyvesant Quartet members
Philharmonia 102

INDY, VINCENT D' (1851-1931)

Fervaal, Opus 40: Introduction to Act I
Westminster Symphony of London, Anatole Fistoulari
MGM E-3062

Fervaal: Introduction to Act I
San Francisco Symphony Orchestra, Monteux, cond.
Victor Album M-1113

Prelude in E Flat Minor
Richard Elsasser, organ
MGM E-3583

IRELAND, JOHN (1879-1962)

Concertino Pastorale: Threnody
MGM String Orchestra, Izler Solomon, cond.
MGM 3074

ISAAC, HEINRICH (c.1450-1517)

La Morra — viols, chalemie, harp, virginal
Nonesuch H-1010

IVES, CHARLES (1874-1954)

Hymn
    Boston Chamber Ensemble, Harold Farberman, cond.
    Cambridge CRM-804

Symphony No. 2: Mvt. II
    The Vienna Orchestra, F. Charles Adler, cond.
    SPA-39

The Unanswered Question
    Zimbler Sinfonietta, Lukas Foss, cond.
    Siena 100-2

JANACEK, LEOS (1854-1928)

Suite for String Orchestra: Mvts. II, V
    Vienna Symphony, Henry Swoboda, cond.
    Westminster 18069

JENKINS, JOHN (1592-1678)

Fancies; Ayres: Ayre (Almaine)
               Ayre (sarabande)
               Ayre in G Minor
               Fancy in C Minor
               Fancy in G Minor
               Pavan in G MInor
    Oxford Chamber Players, Raymond Clauson, cond.
    London Argo RG-73

JERGER, WILHELM (1902-   )

Salzburg Court and Baroque Music (19380;) Courant (in part)
    Hellbrunner Wasserspiele
    Domkonzert
    Bamberger Symphony Orchestra, Wilhelm Jerger, cond.
    Mace 9035

JOLIVET, ANDRÉ (1905-   )

Andante for Strings
    Champs Élysées Theatre Orchestra, Ernest Bour, cond.
    Westminster 5239

Concerto for Harp and Chamber Orchestra: Mvt. II
    Lilly Laskine, harp
    National Opera Orchestra, André Jolivet, cond.
    Westminster 18360

Concerto for Ondes Martenot and Orchestra: Mvt. III
    Martenot, National Opera Orchestra, André Jolivet, cond.
    Westminster 18360

Pastorales de Noel: Mvts. I, II, III
    Philadelphia Woodwind Quintet Members
    Columbia ML-5984

Suite Transoceane: Mvt. III
    The Louisville Orchestra, Robert Whitney, cond.
    Louisville LOU-572

JONGEN, JOSEF (1873-1953)

Legende, Opus 89, No. 1
    New York Philharmonic Cello Quartet

KABALEVSKY, DMITRI (1904-   )

Concerto in C Major for Violin, Opus 48: Mvt. III
    David Oistrakh, violin
    National Philharmonic, Kabalevsky, cond.
    Westminster 18177

KABALEVSKY, DMITRI (Cont.)

Symphony No. 4: Mvt. II
 Leningrad Philharmonic, Kabalevsky, cond.
 Monitor MC-2007

KARLOWICZ, MIECZYSLAW (1876-1909)

Concerto for Violin in A Major, Opus 8: Mvt. II
 Galina Barinova, violin
 USSR State Symphony, Kiril Kondrashin, cond.
 Westminster 18535

KELLER, HOMER (1915-   )

Serenade for Clarinet and Strings
 Eastman-Rochester Orchestra, Howard Hanson, cond.
 Mercury MG-50076

Three Pieces for Strings: Pastorale, Lament
 Radio Eireann Symphony, Milan Horvat, cond.
 Decca 9844

KENNAN, KENT (1913-   )

Night Solilogy for Flute and Strings
 Joseph Mariano, flute
 Eastman-Rochester Orchestra, Howard Hanson, cond.
 Mercury MG-50076

Three Pieces for Orchestra: Nocturne
 Eastman-Rochester Orchestra, Howard Hanson, cond.
 Mercury MG-50147 stereo 90147

KHRENNIKOV, TIKHON (1913-   )

Concerto for Violin in C Major, Opus 14: Mvt. II
 Leonid Kogan, violin
 USSR Radio Orchestra, Kiril Kondrashin, cond.
 MK-1575

KODALY, ZOLTAN (1882-1967)

Peacock Variations (in part)
 Chicago Symphony Orchestra, Antal Dorati, cond.
 Mercury MG-50038

Summer Night
 Budapest Philharmonic Orchestra, Zoltan Kodaly, cond.
 DDG LPM-18 687

KOHS, ELLIS B. (1916-   )

Symphony No. 1 (1950): Mvt. II
 The Vienna Orchestra, F. Charles Adler, cond.
 Composers Recordings, Inc. CRI-104

KRAUS, JOSEPH MARTIN (1756-1792)

Quartet in A Major: Mvt. II
 Mozarteum-Quartett Salzburg
 Musical Heritage MHS-662

Symphony in C Minor: Mvt. II
 Angelicum Orchestra of Milan, Newell Jenkins, cond.
 Nonesuch H-71156

KREUTZER, CONRADIN (1780-1849)

Septet in E Flat Major, Opus 62: Mvts. II, IV
 Vienna Octet Members
 London LL-420

LAJTHA, LASZLO (1891-   )

Quartet No. 7 for Strings, Opus 49 (1950): Mvt. II
 Paganini String Quartet
 Decca 9823

LALANDE, MICHEL-RICHARD DE (1657-1726)
Symphonies for the King's Suppers:
        Sarabande de "Cardenio"
        Musette du ballet de L'Inconnu
        La Pagode
        Jean-Francois Paillard Chamber Orchestra
        Musical Heritage MHS-570

LAMBERT, CONSTANT (1905-1951)
Horoscope, Ballet Suite: Sarabande
        London Philharmonic, Robert Irving, cond.
        London LL-771

LARCHET, JOHN F. (1884-   )
The Dirge of Ossian
        Radio Eireann Orchestra, Milan Horvat, cond.
        Decca 9844

LARSSON, LARS-ERIK (1908-   )
Pastorale Suite: Mvt. II
        Stockholm Symphony, Stig Westerberg, cond.
        London CM-9430   stereo 6430

The Disguised God (lyric suite): Prelude
        Stockholm Radio Symphony, Stig Westerberg, cond.
        Westminster 18528

LAWES, WILLIAM (1602-1645)
Fantazia-Ayre
        Leonhardt-Consort
        Telefunken SAWT 9481

LECLAIR, JEAN-MARIE (1679-1764)
Concerto for Flute and Strings in C Major: Mvt. II
        Camillo Wanausek, flute
        Vienna Pro Musica Orchestra, F. Charles Adler, cond.
        Vox PL-10150

Concerto for Oboe in C Major, No. 3: Mvt. II
        Heinz Holliger, oboe
        Orchestre de Chambre Romand, Alain Milhaud, cond.
        Monitor MC-2091

Concerto for Violin in A Minor, Opus 7, No. 5: Mvt. II
Concerto for Violin in B Flat Major, Opus 10, No. 1: Mvt. II
        Germaine Raymond, violin
        Leclair Instrumental Ensemble, Jean-Francois Paillard
        Haydn Society 9059

Concerto for Violin in E Minor, Opus 10, No. 5: Mvt. II
        Huguette Fernandez, violin
        Leclair Instrumental Ensemble, Jean-Francois Paillard
        Haydn Society 9059

Sonata in D Major, Opus 2, No. 8: Sarabande
Sonata in D Minor, Opus 4, No. 3: Mvts. I, III, IV
        Maxence Larrieu Instrumental Quartet
        Musical Heritage Society MHS-CC2

Sonata for Flute and Harpsichord in B Minor: Mvt. I
Sonata for Flute and Harpsichord in C Major: Mvt. I
Sonata for Flute and Harpsichord in E Minor: Mvts. I, III
Sonata for Flute and Harpsichord in G Major: Mvts. I, III
        Rampl, flute; Veyron-Lacroix, harpsichord
        Oiseau Lyre OL-50051

Sonata for Flute, Harp and Cello: Mvts. I, III
        Members of The Baroque Chamber Ensemble
        Baroque BU-2821

LECLAIR, JEAN-MARIE (Cont.)

Sonata for Flute, Violin and Continuo: Mvt. III
    The Baroque Chamber Ensemble
    Baroque 1803

Sonata for Violin and Continuo: Mvt. I
    Ulrich Grehling, violin;
    Fritz Neumeyer, harpsichord
    Helidor HS 25018

LEES, BENJAMIN (1924-   )

Quartet No. 1 for Strings: Mvt. II
    Juilliard String Quartet
    Epic LC-3325

LEGRENZI, GIOVANNI (1626-1690)

Sonata for Four Violas de Gamba
    Camerata Lutetiensis
    Nonesuch HC-73014

Sonata for Four Violas de Gamba
    The Concentus Musicus, Nikolaus Harnoncourt
    Bach Guild BG-690   stereo 70690

Sonata for Two Violins, Cello, Continuo in D Major
    Musica Sacra AMS-46

LEO, LEONARDO (1694-1744)

Concerto for Cello in A Major: Mvt. III
    Boettcher, cello
    Berlin Chamber Music Circle, Lange, cond.
    Archive ARC 73240

Concerto for Cello in D Major: Mvt. II
    Scarlatti Orchestra of Naples, Franco Caracciolo, cond.
    Angel 35254

LIADOV, ANATOL (1855-1914)

Enchanted Lake
    Bamberg Symphony Orchestra, Jonel Perlea, cond.
    Vox PL-10280

Eight Russian Folk Songs, Opus 58: Lament, Berceuse
    Philharmonia Orchestra, Nicolai Malko, cond.
    Angel 35594

LISZT, FRANZ (1811-1886)

Dante Symphony: Inferno (in part)
                 Purgatorio (in part)
    Budapest Philharmonic, György Lehel, cond.
    Westminster WST-14152

Die Ideale (in part)
    Slovak Philharmonic Orchestra, Ludovit Rajter, cond.
    Parliament PLPS-171

Faust Symphony:
    Royal Philharmonic Orchestra, Sir Thomas Beecham, cond.
    Capitol GBR-7197   stereo SGBR-7197

Mountain Symphony: (two excerpts)
    Berlin Radio Symphony Orchestra, Arthur Rother, cond.
    Urania UR-7091

LOCATELLI, PIETRO (1695-1764)

Concerti Grossi, Opus 1 — No. 2 in C Minor: Mvt. II
                       No. 8 in F Major: Mvts. I, III, IV
                       No. 9 in D Major: Mvt. III
    I Musici, Dean Eckertsen, cond.
    Vox DL-333

LOCATELLI, PIETRO (Cont.)

L'arte del violino, Opus 3, No. 3 in F Major: Mvt. II
    Susanna Lautenbacker, violin
    Mainz Chamber Orchestra, Günter Kehr, cond.
    Vox-500

L'arte del violino, Opus 3, No. 5 in C Major: Mvt. II
                 No. 6 in G Minor: Mvt. II
    Susanna Lautenbacker, violin
    Mainz Chamber Orchestra, Günter Kehr, cond.
    Vox 500-3

L'arte del violino, Opus 3, No. 10 in F Major: Mvt. III
                 No. 11 in A Minor: Mvt. III
    Susanna Lautenbacher, violin
    Mainz Chamber Orchestra, Günter Kehr, cond.
    Vox VBX-41

Il Pianto d'Arianna (excerpts)
    Angelicum Orchestra of Milan, Newell Jenkins, cond.
    Nonesuch H-71151

LOCKE, MATTHEW (c. 1630-1677)

Consorts a Four (Six Suites):
        Suite in D Minor for Four Viols
        Suite in G Major for Four Viols
    Elizabeth Consort of Viols, Dennis Nesbitt, director
    Westminster XWN-19082   stereo 17082

LOCKWOOD, NORMAND (1906-   )

Concerto for Organ and Brasses: Mvt. II
    Soloists, Marilyn Mason, organ
    Remington 199-173

Quiet Design
    Marilyn Mason, organ
    Remington 199-173

LOEILLET, JEAN BAPTISTE (1688-17 ?)

Trio Sonata in C Minor, No. 5: Mvts. I, III
    Pierre Poulteau, recorder
    Andre Chevalet, oboe
    Yvonne Schmit, harpsichord
    Music Guild MG-113

LOEILLET, JEAN BAPTISTE (JOHN) (1680-1730)

Sonata in E MInor: Sarabande
    Piquet, oboe; Lange, bassoon; Rogg, harpsichord
    Odyssey 32 16 0049   stereo 32 16 0050

Sonata in G for Oboe: Mvt. III
    Pierre Pierlot, oboe
    Oiseau Lyre OL-50147

LOPATNIKOV, NIKOLAI (1903-   )

Concertino for Orchestra: Mvt. II
    Columbia Symphony, Leonard Bernstein, cond.
    Columbia ML-4996

LUPO, THOMAS (unknown — 16th Century)

Fantasia
    Leonhard Consort
    Telefunken AWT-9461

Fantasia in B Flat (alto, tenor, bassoon)
    Martha Bixler, Eric Leber, Morris Newman
    Trio Flauto Dolce I

LO PRESTI, RONALD (1933-   )
Suite for Eight Horns: Mvt. II
Horn Club of Los Angeles
Capitol SP-8528

LULLY, JEAN BAPTISTE (1632-1687)
Ballet Music for "Xerxes": Mvts. I, IV
Prague Pro Arte Antiqua Consort of Viols
Bach Guild 591   stereo S-5019

Le Triomphe de l'Amour: Nocturne (arr. Stokowski)
Leopold Stokowski and orchestra
Victor LM-1875*

MACDOWELL, EDWARD (1861-1908)
Suite No. 2, Opus 48 ("Indian"): Dirge
Eastman-Rochester Orchestra, Howard Hanson, cond.
Mercury MG-50082   stereo 90422

MAHLER, GUSTAV (1860-1911)
Symphony No. 2 in C Minor, "Resurrection" (1894): Andante sostenuto
New York Philharmonic Orchestra, Bruno Walter, cond.
Columbia M2L-256   stereo M2S-0601

Symphony No. 4 in C Sharp Minor (1902): Mvt. IV
Vienna State Opera Orchestra, Hermann Scherchen, cond.
Westminster 2220

Symphony No. 6 in A Minor (1904): Mvt. II
Rotterdam Philharmonic, Eduard Flipse, cond.
2-Epic SC-6012

Symphony No. 9 in D Major (1909): Mvt. IV
Vienna Symphony Orchestra, Jascha Horenstein, cond.
3-Vox VBX-116

MAILMAN, MARTIN (1932-   )
Autumn Landscape
Eastman-Rochester Orchestra, Howard Hanson, cond.
Mercury MG-50053*   stereo 90053*

MANFREDINI, FRANCESCO (c. 1680-1748)
Concerti for Two Violins and Strings, Opus 3:
No. 3 in E Minor: Mvt. II
No. 7 in G Major: Mvt. II
No. 10 in G Minor: Mvts. I, III
No. 12 in C Major: Mvts. I, II
Roberto Michelucci, Anna Maria Cotogni, violins
I Musici
Epic LC-3514

MARAIS, MARIN (1656-1728)
Aria
Stuttgart Viol Trio
Janus 19013

Première Suite en ré mineur: Mvts. I, III, V
Bernard Excavi, violoncello
Orchestre de Chambre Jean-Louis Petit
Soc. Francaise du Son SXL 20.117

------

*Music for Quiet Listening Album
*Restful Good Music album

MARCELLO, ALESSANDRO (1684-1750)
Concerti, "La Cetra" — No. 2 in E Major: Mvt. II
No. 6 in G Major: Mvt. II
I Musici
Epic LC-3380

MARCELLO, BENEDETTO (1686-1739)
Aria for Strings in A Minor
Virtuosi di Roma, Renato Fasano, cond.
Decca 9598

Concerto for Oboe and Strings in C Minor: Mvt. II
Harry Shulman, oboe
Daniel Saidenberg Orchestra
Kapp 9041 stereo 9041-S

Concerto Grossi in F Major, Opus 1, No. 4: Mvt. III
I Musici
Angel 35088

Sonata No. 2 in D Minor for Flute and Clavicembalo: Mvt. I
Sonata No. 10 in A Minor for Flute and Clavicembalo: Mvt. I
Arrigo Tassinari, flute
Riccardo Tora, clavicembalo
Period TE 1042

MARCHAND, LOUIS (1669-1732)
Recit en ré
Pierre Froidebise, organ
Nonesuch H-1020

MARESCOTTI, ANDRE-FRANCOIS (1902-   )
L'Aubade: Cantilène
Orchestre de la Suisse Romande, Ernest Ansermet, cond.
Swiss HMV HEX-116-7

MARINI, BIAGIO (? - 1665)
Balleto Secondo: Corrente, Pertirata
Leonhardt Consort
Telefunken AWT-9461

MAROS, RUDOLF (1917-   )
Symphonie pour Orchestre a cordes: Mvt. II
Hungarian Radio Symphony Orchestra, György Lehel
Qualiton LPX 1144

MARTIN, FRANK (1890-   )
Etudes for String Orchestra (1956):
No. 3 "Pour l'expression et le 'Sostenuto' "
Orchestre de la Suisse Romande, Ansermet, cond.
London CM-9310 stereo 6241

MARTINU, BOHUSLAV (1890-1959)
Concerto for Oboe and Orchestra (1955): Mvt. II
Frantisek Hantak, oboe
Brno Philharmonic Orchestra, Martin Turnovsky
Parliament PLP-606 stereo (S) 606

Concerto for Violin (1943): Mvts. I, II
Bruno Belcik, violin
Prague Symphony Orchestra, Vaclav Neumann, cond.
Artia ALP-205

MARTUCCI, GIUSEPPE (1856-1909)
Notturno in G Flat Major, Opus 70, No. 1
London Symphony Orchestra, Pierino Gamba, cond.
London LL-1671

MASSAINO, TIBURTIO (16th - 17th centuries)
Cazon XXXV (plus fragment)
Schola Cantorum Basiliensis, Wenzinger, cond.
Archive ARC 3154

MASSENET, JULES (1842-1912)
Les Erinnyes: No. 2 — Scène Religieuse
No. 3 — Invocation
No. 6 — La Troyenne regrettant sa Patrie
Paris Opera Orchestra, André Cluytens, cond.
Vox PL-8100

Last Sleep Of The Virgin
Royal Philharmonic Orchestra, Sir Thomas Beecham, cond.
Columbia ML-5321

Scenes Alsaciennes: No. 3 — Under The Lindens
Paris Conservatory Orchestra, Albert Wolff, cond.
London CS-6139   stereo STS-15033

MATCHAVARIÁNI, ALEXEI (1913-   )
Concerto for Violin: Mvt. II
Mikhail Vaiman, violin
USSR State Radio Orchestra, Odyssei Dmitriadi, cond.
Westminster 18535

MATTHESON, JOHANN (1681-1764)
Aria in E Minor
E. Power Biggs, organ
Columbia ML-4600

MAY, FREDERICK (1911-   )
Suite of Irish Airs: No. 1 — "An Sparainin"
Radio Eireann Symphony, Milan Horvat, cond.
Decca 9843

MC CAULEY, WILLIAM (1917-   )
Five Miniatures for Flute and Strings: Nos. 2 and 4
Eastman-Rochester Orchestra, Howard Hanson, cond.
Mercury MG-50277   stereo SR-90277

MC KAY, NEIL (1924-   )
Larghetto
Eastman-Rochester Orchestra, Howard Hanson, cond.
Mercury MG-50053*   stereo SR-90053*

MENDELSSOHN, FELIX (1809-1847)
A Midsummer Night's Dream: Nocturne
Amsterdam Concertgebouw, George Szell, cond.
Epic LC-3433

Octet for Strings in E Flat Major: Mvt. II
The Vienna Octet
London CM-9076

Quartet No. 1 for Strings in E Flat Major, Opus 12: Mvt. II
Curtis String Quartet
Westminster 18503

Quartet No. 2 for Strings in A Minor, Opus 13: Mvt. II
Juillard String Quartet
Epic LC-3887

Quartet No. 3 for Strings in D Major, Opus 44, No. 1: Mvt. III
Curtis String Quartet
Westminster 18503

————————
*Music for Quiet Listening album

MENDELSSOHN, FELIX (Cont.)

Quartet No. 3 for Strings in D Major, Opus 44, No. 1: Mvt. III
Juilliard String Quartet
Epic LC-3887

Quartet No. 5 for Strings in E Flat Major, Opus 44, No. 3: Mvt. III
Endres String Quartet
Stradivari 615

Quartet No. 6 for Strings in F Minor, Opus 80: Mvt. III
Manoliu String Quartet
Epic LC-3386

String Symphony in B Minor: Adagio
String Symphony in G Minor: Andante
Vienna Opera Orchestra, Mathieu Lange, cond.
VOX PL-14205

String Sinfonia No. 9: Mvt. II
Winograd String Orchestra, Arthur Winogard, cond.
Heliodor HS 25021

Sonata No. 1 for Organ in F Minor: Mvt. II
E. Power Biggs
Columbia ML-5409   stereo MCS 6087

Sonata No. 3 for Organ in A Major: Mvt. II
John Davis
Vox VX-25800   stereo 14030

MENDOZA-NAVA, JAIME (1925-   )

Estampas y Estampillas: No. 2—"Don Andalu", No. 4—"Siesta"
MGM Orchestra, Carlos Surinach, cond.
MGM 3513

MENNIN, PETER (1923-   )

Quartet No. 2 for Strings: Mvt. II
Juilliard String Quartet
Columbia ML-4844

Symphony No. 3: Mvt. II
New York Philharmonic, Dimitri Mitropoulos, cond.
Columbia ML-4902

Symphony No. 6: Mvt. II
The Louisville Orchestra, Robert Whitney, cond.
Louisville LOU-5453

MENNINI, LOUIS (1920-   )

Arioso for Strings
Eastman-Rochester Orchestra, Howard Hanson, cond.
Mercury MG-50074

MESSIAEN, OLIVER (1908-   )

L'Ascension: Mvts. II, IV
Le Banquet Céleste
Les Corps Glorieux: Mvts. I, IV, VII
Diptyque: part two
La Nativite du Seigneur: Mvts. I, II, III, IV (in part), V (in part), VII
Oliver Messiaen, organ
Ducretet-Thomson 260 C 074/260 C 081

MIASKOVSKY, NICOLAI (1881-1950)

Concerto for Cello in C Major: Mvt. I
Mstislav Rostropovich, cello
Philharmonia Orchestra, Sir Malcolm Sargent, cond.
Victor LM-2016

MIASKOVSKY, NICOLAI (Cont.)

Concerto for Violin in D Minor: Mvt. II
David Oistrakh, violin — Symphony
Orchestra conducted by Alexander Gauk
Period 539

Quartet No. 13 for Strings in A Minor: Mvt. II
The Beethoven Quartet
Westminster 18423

Symphony No. 17 in G Sharp Minor, Opus 41: Mvt. II
USSR State Radio Orchestra, Alexander Gauk, cond.
MK-1575

MÍCA, FRANTÍSEK VÁCLAV (1694-1744)

Symphony in D Major: Mvt. II
Prague Symphony Orchestra, Václav Smetacke, cond.
Supraphone MAB-2

MILHAUD, DARIUS (1892-   )

Concerto No. 1 for Cello: Mvt. II
Janos Starker, cello
Philharmonia Orchestra, Walter Süsskind, cond.
Angel 35418   stereo S-35418

Deux Esquisses: Mvt. I
La Cheminée Du Roi René: Madrigal (in part)
Wind Quintet of the French National Radio Orchestra
Angel 35079

Household Muse Suite: La Mienne, La. Poesie,
Reconnaissance a la Musa
Vienna Philharmonic, Herbert Haefner, cond.
SPA-12

Quartet No. 1 for Strings: Mvt. II
WQXR String Quartet
Polymusic 1004

Quartet No. 12 for Strings: Mvt. II
Quartetto Italiano
Angel 35130

Rag Caprices: No. 2 — "Romance"
Vienna Symphony, Henry Swoboda, cond.
Westminster 18717

Sketches for Woodwind Quintet: Madrigral
New York Woodwind Quintet
Esoteric 505

MITYUSHIN, ALEXANDER (1888-   )

Concertino for Four Horns (1952): Mvt. II
Chicago Symphony Horn Quartet
Concert Disc M-1243   stereo 243

MOERAN, ERNEST JOHN (1894-   )

Trio for Strings in G Major: Mvt. II
Jean Pougnet, violin; Frederick Riddle, viola
Anthony Pini, cello
English Columbis DX-8153/5

MONN, GEORG (1717-1750)

Quartetto I in B Flat Major: Mvt. I
Concentus Musicus, Wien, cond.
Telefunken SAWT 9475

MONTEVERDI, CLAUDIO (1567-1643)

Three Madrigals: Ardo si ma non t'amo
Ardi o gela
Arsi e alsi
Camerata Lutetiensis
Nonesuch HC-73014

MOOR, EMANEUL (1863-1931)

Suite for Four Cellos, Opus 95 (1909): Mvt. III
New York Philharmonic Cello Quartet
Decca 9946

MOORE, DOUGLAS (1893-   )

Farm Journal (1947): "Lamp Light"
Oslo Philharmonic Orchestra, Alfredo Antonini, cond.
Composers Recordings, Inc. CRI-101

Quintet for Clarinet and Strings (1946): Mvt. II
David Oppenheim, clarinet
New Music String Quartet
Columbia ML-4494

Symphony No. 2 in A Major (1946): Mvt. II
Japan Philharmonic Orchestra, William Strickland, cond.
Composers Recordings, Inc. CRI-133

MOULINIÉ, ETIENNE (c. 1600-1669)

Fantasie No. 1
Viol Quartet, Schola Cantorum Basiliensis
Musical Heritage MHS 598

MOURANT, WALTER (1910-   )

Sleepy Hollow Suite:
In The Valley of The Moon: Air
New Symphony Orchestra, Camarata, cond.
London LL-1213

MOURET, JEAN-JOSEPH (1682-1738)

Concert de Chambre in E Major: Mvt. VI
Orchestre de Chambre, Gerard Cartigny, cond.
Music Guild M-18   stereo (s) 106

Les amans ignorans: Air Turc
La Foire des Fees: Air pour les Fees et les amans
L'amante difficile: Sommeil, Menuets
Orchestre de Chambre, Jean Louis Petit, cond.
Soc. Francaise du Son SXL 20-130

MOZART, WOLFGANG AMADEUS (1756-1791)

Adagio in E Major, K. 261
Nap DeKlijn, violin
Vienna Symphony, Bernard Paumgartner, cond.
Epic LC-3197

Adagio for Glass Harmonica, K. 356
E. Power Biggs, organ
Columbia ML-4331

Adagio in F Major for String Trio, K. 404a
Pasquier Trio
Haydn Society 108

Adagio in D Minor, K. 404a
Adagio in G Minor, K. 404a
Janssen Symphony of Los Angeles, Werner Janssen, cond.
Columbia ML-4406

MOZART, WOLFGANG AMADEUS (Cont.)

Adagio in B Flat Major, K. 440
    Michaels, Stute, clarinets
    Irmisch, Helmke, Peppler, basset horns
    Archive 3121

Adagio for English Horn, Two Violins and Cello, K. 580a
    London Baroque Ensemble
    Decca 4055

Cassation No. 1 in G Major. K. 63: Mvts. III, IV
    Zimbler Sinfonietta
    Decca 3204

Concerto in B Flat Major for Bassoon, K. 191: Mvt. II
    Gwydion Brooke, bassoon
    Royal Philharmonic Orchestra, Sir Thomas Beecham, cond.
    Capitol G-7201   stereo SG-7201

Concerto in B Flat Major for Bassoon, K. 191: Andante
    Rudolf Klepac, Bassoon
    Mozarteun Orchestra of Salzburg, Ernest Marzendorfer, cond.
    Decca DL-9834

Concerto for Clarinet in A Major, K. 622: Mvt. II
    Jack Brymer, clarinet
    Royal Philharmonic Orchestra, Sir Thomas Beecham, cond.
    Capitol G-7021   stereo SG-7201

Concerto for Flute in G Major, K. 313: Mvt. II
Concerto for Flute in D Major, K. 314: Mvt. II
    Camillo Wanausek, flute
    Vienna Pro Musica Orchestra
    Vox PL-8550

Concerto No. 2 in D Major for Flute, K. 314: Mvt. II
    Elaine Schaffer, flute
    Philharmonia Orchestra, Efrem Kurtz, cond.
    Capitol G-7135

Concerto for Flute and Harp in C Major, K. 299: Mvt. II
    Camillo Wanasuek, flute;
    Hurbert Jellinek, harp;
    Vienna Pro Musica Orchestra
    Vox PL-8550

Concerto No. 4 for Horn in E Flat Major, K. 495: Mvt. II
    Dennis Brain, horn
    Philharmonia Orchestra, Herbert Von Karajan, cond.
    Angel 35092

Concerto No. 3 for Violin in G Major, K. 216: Mvt. II
Concerto No. 4 for Violin in D Major, K. 218: Mvt. II
    Szymon Goldberg, violin
    Philharmonia Orchestra, Walter Süsskind, cond.
    Decca 9609

Concerto No. 5 for Violin in A Major, K. 219: Mvt. II
    Arthur Grumiaux, violin
    Vienna Symphony Orchestra, Bernard Paumgartner, cond.
    Epic LC-3157

Concerto No. 6 for Violin in E Flat Major, K. 268: Mvt. II
    Christian Ferras, violin
    Stuttgart Chamber Orchestra, Karl Münchinger, cond.
    London LL-1172

Concertone, K. 190: Mvt. II
    Hurwitz, Goren, violins; Graeme, oboe; Weil, cello
    English Chamber Orchestra, Colin Davis, cond.
    Oiseau-Lyre 50199   stereo SOL-60030

MOZART, WOLFGANG AMADEUS (Cont.)

Divertimenti for Clarinets and Bassoon, K.Anh 229 (439b):
    No. 1: Mvt. III
    No. 4: Mvts. II, IV
  Pierlot, oboe; Lancelot, clarinet;
  Hongne, bassoon
  Musical Heritage MHS-605

Divertimento for Clarinets and Bassoon, No. 3, K.439b: Adagio
  Vienna Symphony Wind Group
  Epic LC-3081

Divertimento in B Flat Major, K. 137: Mvt. II
Divertimento in F Major, K. 138: Mvt. I
  I Musici
  Epic LC-3813

Divertimento No. 1 in E Flat Major, K. 113: Mvt. II
  Bamberg Symphony, Joseph Keilberth, cond.
  Telefunken TC-8032   stereo 18032

Divertimento No. 2 in D Major, K. 131: Mvt. II
  Royal Philharmonic Sir Thomas Beecham, cond.
  Angel 35459

Divertimento No. 7 in D Major, K. 205: Mvt. III
  Salzburg Mozarteum Orchestra, Marzendorfer, cond.
  London LL-1427

Divertimento No. 8 in F Major, K. 213: Mvt. II
  Vienna Philharmonic Wind Group
  Westminster 18552

Divertimento No. 10 in F Major, K. 247: Mvt. IV
  Members of the Vienna Octet
  London LPS-682   stereo-6379

Divertimento No. 11 in D Major, K. 251: Mvt. III
  Suttgart Chamber Orchestra, Karl Münchinger, cond.
  London CS-6169   stereo STS 15035

Divertimento No. 12 in E Flat Major, K. 252: Mvt. I
  Vienna Philharmonic Winds, Bernhard Paumgartner
  Epic LC-3081

Divertimento No. 13 in F Major, K. 253: Mvt. I
  Vienna Philharmonic Winds, Bernhard Paumgartner, cond.
  Epic LC-3081

Divertimento No. 15 in B Flat Major, K. 287: Mvt. IV
  Philharmonia Orchestra, Herbert Von Karajan, cond.
  Angel 35563

Divertimento No. 16 in E Flat Major, K. 289: Mvt. III
  Vienna Philharmonic Winds, Bernhard Paumgartner, cond.
  Epic LC-3081

Divertimento No. 17 in D Major, K. 334: Mvt. IV
  Veinna State Opera Orchestra, Felix Prohaska, cond.
  Vanguard 441

Divertimento for String Trio, K. 563: Mvt. II
  Jean Pougnet, Frederick Riddle, Anthony Pini
  Westminster 18551

Divertimento in D Major, K. 136: Mvt. II
  Stuttgart Chamber Orchestra, Karl Münchinger, cond.
  London CM-9144   stereo 6207

Fantasia in F Minor for Organ, K. 594: Mvts. I, III
  Marie-Claire Alain, organ
  Westminster 19091   stereo 17091

MOZART, WOLFGANG AMADEUS (Cont.)

Masonic Funeral Music, K. 477
    Columbia Symphony Orchestra, Bruno Walter, cond.
    Columbia ML-5756 stereo MS-6356

Quartets for Flute and Strings, K. 285, 285a, 285b
        No. 1 in D Major: Mvt. II
        No. 2 in G Major: Mvt. I
        No. 3 in C Major: Mvt. II
    Poul Birkelund, flute; Arne Karecki, violin
    Herman Andersen, viola; Alf Petersen, cello
    Vanguard 1006

Quartet for Oboe and Strings in F Major, K. 370: Mvt. II
    Marcel Tabuteau, oboe; Isaac Stern, violin
    William Primrose, viola; Paul Tortellier, cello
    Columbia ML-4566

Quartet No. 1 for Strings in G Major, K. 80: Mvt. I
Quartet No. 2 for Strings in D Major, K. 155: Mvt. II
Quartet No. 3 for Strings in G Major, K. 156: Mvt. II
Quartet No. 4 for Strings in C Major, K. 157: Mvt. II
Quartet No. 7 for Strings in E Flat Major, K. 160: Mvt. II
Quartet No. 8 for Strings in F Major, K. 168: Mvt. II
Quartet No. 10 for Strings in C Major, K. 170: Mvt. III
    Barchet String Quartet
    Vox VBX 12

Quartet No. 12 for Strings in B Flat Major, K. 172: Mvt. II
Quartet No. 14 for Strings in G Major, K. 387: Mvt. III
Quartet No. 15 for Strings in D Minor, K. 421: Mvt. II
    Barchet String Quartet
    Vox VBX-13

Quartet No. 16 for Strings in E Flat Major, K. 428: Mvt. II
Quartet No. 17 for Strings in B Flat Major, K. 458: Mvt. II
    Budapest String Quartet
    Columbia ML-4727

Quartet No. 19 for Strings in C Major, K. 465: Mvt. II
    Budapest String Quartet
    Columbia ML-4728

Quartet No. 20 for Strings in D Major, K. 499: Mvt. III
Quartet No. 21 for STrings in D Major, K. 575: Mvt. II
    Budapest String Quartet
    Columbia ML-5007

Quartet No. 22 for Strings in B Flat Major, K. 589: Mvt. II
    Budapest String Quartet
    Columbia ML-5008

Quartet for Strings in C Major, K. Anh. 211: Mvt. II
    Barchet String Quartet
    Vox PL-7489

Quintet in B Flat Major, K. 46 (from Serenade No. 10): Mvt. III
    Pascal String Quartet; Walter Gerhard 2nd Viola
    Record Hunter Rarities Collection RC-307

Quintet in B Flat Major, K. 174: Mvt. II
    Budapest String Quartet, Walter Trampler, 2nd Viola
    Columbia ML-5191

Quintet in C Major, K. 515: Mvt. III
    Budapest String Quartet; Walter Trampler, 2nd Viola
    Columbia ML-5192

Quintet for Clarinet and Strings in A Major, K. 581: Mvt. II
    David Oppenheim, clarinet
    Budapest String Quartet
    Columbia ML-5455 stereo MS-6127

MOZART, WOLFGANG AMADEUS (Cont.)

Quintet for Horn and String in E Flat, K. 407: Mvt. II
Fine Arts Quartet; John Barrows, horn
Concert-Disc 1204   stereo 203

Serenade No. 4 in D Major, K. 203 (189b): Mvts, III, VII
Cappella Coloniensis, Ferdinand Leitner, cond.
Archive ARC 73263

Serenade No. 7 in D Major ("Haffner"), K. 250: Mvt. II
Vienna Philharmonic Orchestra, Karl Münchinger, cond.
London CM-9283   stereo 6214

Serenade No. 8 in D Major for Four Orchestras, K. 286: Mvt. I
Bamberg Symphony Orchestra, Joseph Keilberth, cond.
Telefunken TC-8032   stereo 18032

Serenade No. 9 in D Major, ("Posthorn Serenade"), K. 320: Mvt. III
Barylli Quartet and Vienna Philharmonic Wind Group
Westminster 18033

Serenade No. 10 in B Flat for 13 Wind Instruments, K. 361: Mvt. III
Eastman Wind Ensemble, Frederick Fennell, cond.
Mercury 90412

Serenade No. 11 in E Flat Major, K. 375: Mvt. II
Everest Woodwind Octet, Newell Jenkins, cond.
Everest 6042   stereo 3042

Serenade No. 12 in C Minor, K. 388: Mvt. II
Everest Woodwind Octet, Newell Jenkins, cond.
Everest 6042   stereo 3042

Serenade in D Major, K. 185: Mvt. II
Austrian Tonkuenstler Orchestra, Lee Schaen, cond.
Musical Heritage Society MHS 715

Sinfonia Concertante in E Flat, K. Anh. 9: Mvt. II
The Philadelphia Orchestra, Eugene Ormandy, cond.
Columbia ML-5374   stereo MS-6061

Sonata No. 4 for Flute, K. 13:
Rampal, flute; Veyron Lacroix, harpsichord
Epic BC-1288

Symphony in F Major, K. 75: Mvt. III
Symphony in D Minor, K. 81: Mvt. II
Symphony in D Major, K. 95: Mvt. II
Austrian Tonkuenstler Orchestra, Ernest Maerzendorfer, cond.
Musical Heritage Society MHS-663

Symphony in C Major, K. 96: Mvt. II
Symphony in D Major, K. 120: Mvt. II
Austrian Tonkuenstler Orchestra, Ernest Maerzendorfer, cond.
Musical Heritage Society MHS-702

Symphony No. 3, K. 18: Andante (in part)
Netherlands Philharmonic Orchestra, Otto Ackermann, cond.
Record Hunter CHS-1178

Symphony No. 4 in D Major, K. 19: Mvt. II
Netherlands Philharmonic Orchestra, Otto Ackermann, cond.
Reocrd Hunter Rarities Collection RC-1166

Symphony No. 6 in F Major, K. 43: Mvt. II
Netherlands Philharmonic Orchestra, Otto Ackermann, cond.
Record Hunter Rarities Collection RC-1165

Symphony No. 14 in A Major, K. 114: Mvt. II
London Philharmonic Orchestra, Erich Leinsdorf, cond.
Westminster 18864   stereo 14078

Symphony No. 15 in G Major, K. 124: Mvt. II
London Philharmonic Orchestra, Erich Leinsdorf, cond.
Westminster 18864   stereo 14078

MOZART, WOLFGANG AMADEUS (Cont.)

Symphony No. 17 in G Major, K. 129: Mvt. II
London Philharmonic Orchestra, Erich Leinsdorf, cond.
Westminster 18864 stereo 14078

Symphony No. 20 in D Major, K. 133: Mvt. II
London Philharmonic Orchestra, Erich Leinsdorf, cond.
Westminster 18782 stereo 14097

Symphony No. 22 in C Major, K. 162: Mvt. II
London Philharmonic Orchestra, Erich Leinsdorf, cond.
Westminster 18756 stereo 14756

Symphony No. 24 in E Flat Major, K. 182: Mvt. II
London Philharmonic Orchestra, Erich Leinsdorf, cond.
Westminster 18756 stereo 14756

Symphony No. 29 in A Major, K. 201: Mvt. II
London Philharmonic Orchestra, Erich Leinsdorf, cond.
Westminster 18216 stereo 14216

Symphony No. 33 in B Flat Major, K. 319: Mvt. II
London Philharmonic Orchestra, Erich Leinsdorf, cond.
Westminster 18186 stereo 14186

MOZART-FISCHER

Cello Concerto in E Flat Major, K. 447: Mvt. II
(from Horn Concerto)
Janos Starker, cello
Castle Hills Festival Orchestra, Max Pilzer, cond.
Period TE-1093

MUFFAT, GEORG (1653-1704)

Sonata No. 1 in D Major: Mvt. II
Austrian Tonkuenstler Orchestra, Theodor Guschlbauer, cond.
Musical Heritage MHS-601

Sonata No. 5 from Armonico Tributo: Adagio
Concentus Musicus, Passacaglia, cond.
Bach-Guild BG-652

MULLER, PAUL (1898-   )

Sinfonia No. 2 for Flute and Strings, Opus 53: Mvt. II
Andre Jaunet, flute
Zürich Chamber Orchestra, Edmond de Stoutz, cond.
London LP LLP-1183

NAPRAVNIK, EDUARD (1839-1916)

Don Juan: The Song of the Nightingale
Milan La Scala Orchestra, Panizza, cond.
Victor 9730 (78 rpm)

NARDINI, PIETRO (1722-1793)

Concerto for Violin in E Minor: Mvt. II
Peter Rybar, violin
Winterhur Symphony, Clemens Dahinden, cond.
Westminster 18192

NAUDOT, JEAN-JACQUES (XVIII Century)

Concerto for Oboe in C Major, Opus 17, No. 3: Mvt. II
Leclair Instrumental Ensemble, Jean-Francois Paillard
Haydn Society 103

NELSON, RON

Sarabande — For Katharine in April
Eastman-Rochester Orchestra, Howard Hanson, cond.
Mercury MG-50053* stereo 90053*

_____

*Music for Quiet Listening album

NICODE, JEAN LOUIS (1853-1919)
Carnival Scenes: "Strange Dream" Mvt. III
Symphony of Radio Leipzig, Hilmar Weber, cond.
Urania UR-7122

NIELSON, CARL (1865-1931)
Concerto for Violin, Opus 33, (1912): Mvts. I (in part), II
Tibor Varga, violin
Royal Danish Orchestra, Jerzy Semkow, cond.
Turnabout TV 34043 S

Maskarade: Prelude to Act II
Danish State Radio Orchestra, Thomas Jensen, cond.
London LL-1314

Quartet No. 2 for Strings in F Minor, Opus 5: Mvt. II
Musica Vitalis Quartet
London LL-1078

Quartet No. 2 for Strings in F Minor, Opus 5: Mvt. II
Copenhagen String Quartet
Turnabout 34149 S

Quartet No. 3 for Strings in E Flat Major: Mvt. II
Copenhagen String Quartet
Turnabout TV 34109 S

Quartet for String in F Major, (1906): Mvt. II
Erling Bloch String Quartet
Odeon MOAK-30004

Quintet for Winds, Opus 43: Theme and Variations (in part)
The Philadelphia Woodwind Quintet
Columbia ML-5441   stereo MS-6114

Serenata in Vano (1914) for Clarinet, Bassoon, Horn,
Cello and Bass: In Part
Robert Gardner, Cello
The Lark Woodwind Quintet
Lyrichord LL-155

Symphony No. 2, Opus 16, (1902) "The Four Temperaments": Mvt. II
Tivoli Concert Hall Orchestra, Carl Garaguly, conductor
Turnabout (3) 4049

Three Preludes for Organ
Grethe Krogh Christensen, organ of Holmens, Copenhagen
Lyrichord LL-148

NYSTROEM, GOSTA (1890-   )
The Marchant Of Venice, Suite: Mvt. III, "Nocturne"
Stockholm Radio Orchestra, Tor Mann, cond.
Westminster 18147

PACHELBEL, JOHANN (1653-1706)
The Seven Chorale Partitas —
Christus, der ist mein Leben: Var. 7
Herzlich tut mich verlangen: Var. 1, 4, 5
Was Gott ut ist wohlgetan: Var. 4, 6
Freu dich sehr, O meine Selle: ·Var. 4
Robert Owen, organ
Westminster 18829

PAISELLO, GIOVANNI (1740-1816)
Concerto a Cinque for Strings: Mvt. II
Virtuosi di Roma, Renate Fasano, cond.
Decca 9730

PALESTRINA, GIOVANNI DA (1524-1594)

Adoramus Te (arr. Stokowski)
>Symphony of the Air, Leopold Stokowski, cond.
>United Artists 7001   stereo 8001

Ricercari sopra li toni (8)
>Camerata Lutetiensis
>Nonesuch 73014

Stabat Mater
>Horn Club of Los Angeles
>Capitol SP-8528

PEPUSCH, JOHN CHRISTOPHER (1667-1752)

Sonata for Oboe in D Minor: Mvt. I
>Pierre Pierlot, oboe
>Oiseau Lyre OL-50174

PERGOLESI, GIOVANNI (1710-1736)

Concertini for Strings: No. 1 in G Major: Mvts. I, III
>   No. 2 in G Major: Mvt. II
>   No. 6 in B Flat Major: Mvt. II
>I Musici
>Angel 35251

Concertini for Strings: No. 3 in A Major: Mvts. I, II, III
>   No. 4 in F Minor: Mvt. I
>   No. 5 in E Flat Major: Mvts. I, III
>Winterthur Symphony Orchestra, Angelo Ephrikian, cond.
>Westminster 18587

Concerto in D Major for Flute and Strings: Mvt. III
>Camillo Wanausek, flute
>Vienna Pro Musica Orchestra, Adler, cond.
>Vox PL-10150

Concerto in G Major for Flute and Strings: Mvt. II
>Schaeffer, flute
>N. German Chamber Orchestra, Lange, cond.
>Archive ARC-73240

Concerto in G Major for Flute: Mvt. II
>Jean-Pierre Rampal, flute
>Lesclair Instrumental Ensemble, Paillard, cond.
>Musical Heritage Society MHS-570

Sinfonia for Cello and Strings: Mvts. I, III
>I Musici
>Angel 35251

Sonata for Violin and Strings: Mvt. II
>I Musici
>Angel 35251

PERSICHETTI, VINCENT (1915-   )

Symphony No. 5 for Strings, Opus 61, (1950) Mvt. III
>The Louisville Orchestra, Robert Whitney, cond.
>Louisville LOU-606

Pastorale
>Philadelphia Woodwind Quintet
>Columbia ML-5984

PETRASSI, GOFFREDO (1904-   )

Concerto for Orchestra: Mvt. II
>St. Cecelia Academy Orchestra, Fernando Previtali
>London CM-9173   stereo CS-6112

PEZ, J. C. (PETZ) (1664-1716)
Concerto Pastorale in F Major: Mvts. I, III
    Austrian Tonkuenstler Orchestra, Topolski, cond.
    Musical Heritage MHS 714

PFITZNER, HANS (1869-1949)
Palestrina: Preludes to Acts I and III
    Berlin Philharmonic, Ferdinand Leitner, cond.
    Deutsche-Grammophon LPEM-19176 stereo 136022

PHILIDOR, ANNE DANICAN (1681-1728)
Sonata in D Minor for Flute: Mvt. I
    Rampal, flute
    Vyeron-Lacroix, harpischord
    Dover HCR-5238 stereo 7238

PHILLIPS, BURRILL (1907-)
Selections From McGuffey's Reader (1934): Mvt. II
    Eastman-Rochester Orchestra, Howard Hanson, cond.
    Mercury MG-50136

PIERNÉ, GABRIEL (1863-1937)
Pastorale
    Philadelphia Woodwind Quintet
    Columbia ML-5984

PISTON, WALTER (1894-)
Prelude and Allegro for Organ: Prelude
    Boston Symphony Orchestra, Serge Koussevitsky, cond.
    Victor 11-9262 (78 rpm)

Serenata: Mvt. II
    The Louisville Orchestra, Robert Whitney, cond.
    Louisville LOU-586

Symphony No. 4 (1949): Mvt. III (in part)
    The Philadelphia Orchestra, Eugene Ormandy, cond.
    Columbia ML-4992

Symphony No. 6: Mvt. III
    Boston Symphony Orchestra, Charles Munch, cond.
    Victor LM-2083

PLEYEL, IGNAZ (1757-1813)
Quartet for Flute in D Major, Book 3, No. 1: Mvt. II
    Rampal, flute; Gendre, violin;
    Lepauw, viola; Bex, cello.
    L'Oiseau Lyre OL-50188 stereo 60016

POSCH, ISAAC (Late 16th century—Early 17th Century)
Intrada
    Concentus
    Bach Guild BG-626

POPORA, NICCOLO (1686-1767)
Aria for Cello and Strings
    Benedetto Mazzacurati, cello
    Virtuosi di Roma, Renato Fasano, cond.
    Decca 9731

PORTER, QUINCY (1897-)
Music for Strings
    MGM String Orchestra, Izler Solomon, cond.
    MGM-3117

PROKOFIEV, SERGE (1891-1953)

Cincerella, Ballet Suite: Apotheosis
    Stadium Symphony Orchestra, Leopold Stokowski, cond.
    Everest 6016 stereo 3016

Concerto No. 1 for Violin in D Major, Opus 19, (1913): Mvt. I
    David Oistrakh, violin
    National Philharmonic Orchestra, Serge Prokofiev, cond.
    Period 739

Four Portraits from the Opera "The Gambler," Opus 49:
        1. Alexis
        2. Pauline
    Philharmonic Orchestra of London, William Schuechter, cond.
    MGM E-3112

Love for Three Oranges, Suite: The Prince and the Princess
    London Philharmonic Orchestra, Sir Adrian Boult, cond.
    London CM-9142

Quartet No. 2 in F Major: Mvt. II
    Quartetto Italiano
    Angel 35296

Quartet No. 1 for Strings: Mvt. III
    Guilet String Quartet
    MGM-3113

Romeo and Juliet, Suite: "Juliet," "Love Scene"
    NBC Symphony Orchestra, Leopold Stokowski, cond.
    Victor LM-2117

Sonata for Two Violins: Mvts. I, III
    David and Igor Oistrakh
    Monitor MC-2058

Stone Flower Ballet: Three Movements from Act I
    L'Orchestre de la Suisse Romande
    London CM-9458

Symphony No. 2 in D Minor, Opus 40 (1925): Mvt. II (in part)
    Moscow Radio Symphony Orchestra, Gennady Rozhdestvensky, cond.
    MK-1583

Symphony No. 3, Opus 44 (1928): Mvt. II
    USSR State Symphony Orchestra, Gennady Rozhdestvensky, cond.
    Artia ALP-191

Symphony No. 7, Opus 131: Mvt. III
    Czech Philharmonic Orchestra, Nikolai Anosov, cond.
    Parliament PLP-122

Visions Fugitives, Opus 22 (arr. Barshai): Mvt. I
    Moscow Chamber Orchestra, Barshai
    Angel 35981

Winter Holiday, Opus 122: Winter Nights
                        Evening Around the Stove
                        The Return
    USSR State Radio Orchestra, Samuel Samosud, cond.
    Westminster 18081

PUCCINI, GIACOMO (1858-1924)

Crisantemi (Elegy for String Quartet)
    Quartetto della Scala
    Urania 7074

Manon Lescaut: Act III: Intermezzo
    Philharmonia Orchestra, Herbert Von Karajan, cond.
    Angel 35793 stereo S-35793

PUCCINI, GIACOMO (Cont.)

Suor Angelica: Intermezzo
 Maggio Musicale Fiorentino, Gavazzeni, cond.
 London CM-9177 stereo CS-6121

PURCELL, HENRY (1659-1695)

Fanatsia No. 4 in G Minor: (in part)
Fantasia No. 7 in C Minor: (in part)
 Yehudi Menuhin and Cecil Aronowitz, violins
 Walter Gerhard, viola; Derek Simpson, cello
 Angel 36270

Fantasies for Strings: No. 12 in D Minor
        No. 14 in G Minor
        No. 15 in G Minor
 Gamba Quartet of the Schola Cantorum Basiliensis
 Archive 3007

In Nominee for Six Voices
In Nominee for Seven Voices
 Concentus Musicus, Vienna, Nikolaus Harnoncourt, cond.
 Bach Guild BG-676

Lament of Dido (arr. Stokowski)
 Leopold Stokowski and Orchestra
 Victor LM-1875*

London — Chancony in G Minor
 Vienna Chamber Orchestra, Franz Litschauer
 Vanguard VRS-419

Pavane and Chancony in G Minor
 New Music String Quartet
 Bartok 913

Sonatas of III Parts, No. 1 in G Minor: Mvts. I, III, V
 Neville Mariner and Peter Gibbs, violins
 Desmond Dupre, bass viol; Thurston Dart, organ
 London Argo 209

Sonatas of III Parts: Sonata in A Minor: Largo
       Sonata in D Minor: Mvt. III
       Sonata in F Major: Largo, Andante
 Jacobean Ensemble, Thurston Dart, organ
 Spoken Arts 209 (Vol. I)

Sonatas of III Parts, No. 6 in C Major: (in part)
 Yehudi Menuhin and Alberto Lysy, violins
 Ambrose Gauntlett, viola da gamba
 Roy Jesson, harpsichord
 Angel 36270 stereo S-36270

Sonatas of III Parts, No. 9
 Neville Marriner and Peter Gibbs, violins;
 Desmond Dupre, bass viol, Thurston Dart, organ
 Spoken Arts 210 (Vol. II)

Sonatas of IV Parts: No. 1 in B Minor: Mvt. I
      No. 2 in E Flat Major: Five Movements
      No. 7 in C Major: Mvt. II
      No. 8 in G Minor: Mvt. II
      No. 9 in F Major: Mvts..I, II, IV
      No. 10 in D Major: Five Movements (entire)
 Giorgio Ciompi and Werner Torkanowsky, violins
 George Koutzen cello; Herman Chessid, harpsichord
 Dover HCR-5224

---

*Restful Good Music album.

PURCELL, HENRY (Cont.)

Suite from "The Gordian Knot United": Rondeau
Suite from "The Married Beau":· Slow Air
Suite from "The Virtuous Wife": Slow Air, Minuet I
  Hartford Chamber Orchestra, Fritz Mahler, cond.
  Bach Guild 605   stereo 5032

PURSELL, WILLIAM (1926-   )

Christ Looking Over Jerusalem
  Eastman-Rochester Orchestra, Howard Hanson, cond.
  Mercury MG-50053*   stereo 90053*

QUANTZ, JOHANN JOACHIM (1697-1773)

Concerto for Flute in E Minor: Mvt. II
  Karl-Heinz Zoller, flute
  Berlin Philharmonic Orchestra, Hans van Benda, cond.
  Electrola 91 100   stereo Angel S-36272

Concerto in G Major for Flute and Strings: Mvt. II
  Hubert Barwahser, flute
  Vienna Symphony Orchestra, Bernhard Paumgartner, cond.
  Epic LC-3134

Sonate en Trio in C Minor: Mvts. I, III
  Ensemble Baroque de Paris
  Boite a Musique LD-011

Trio Sonata in C Minor: Mvt. III
  French Chamber Group
  Haydn Society 9026

Trio Sonata in C Minor: Mvts. I, II
  Eichendorf Wind Group
  Musiçal Heritage MHS-581

Trio Sonata in C Major for Flute, Recorder and Continuo: Mvt. I
  Franz Vester, flute; Frans Bruggen, recorder;
  Anner Bylsma, cello; Gustav Leonhardt, cembalo
  Telefunken SAWT 9464

RACHMANINOFF, SERGEI (1873-1943)

Daisies, Opus 38, No. 3
Melodie in E Major, Opus 3, No. 3
Prelude in E Flat Major, Opus 23, No. 6
Prelude in G Major, Opus 32, No. 5
  Andre Kostelanetz and Orchestra
  Columbia CL-1001

Quartet for Strings in G Minor: Romance
  Guilet String Quartet
  MGM-3133

Symphonic Dances (excerpts)
  London Symphony Orchestra, Eugene Goossens
  Everest SDBR-3004   stereo 3151

Vocalise, Opus 34, No. 14
  Leopold Stokowski and Orchestra
  Victor LM-2042

RAKOV, NIKOLAI (1908-   )

Concerto for Violin and Orchestra in E Minor: Mvt. II
  Igor Oistrakh, violin
  National Philharmonic, Rakov, cond.
  Bruno 14017

----

*Music for Quet Listening album.

RAMEAU, JEAN PHILIPPEE (1683-1764)

Acante et Céphise: Danses: Menuet. Mvts. I, II
Caen Chamber Orchestra, Jean-Pierre Dautel, cond.
Turnabout TV 34101-S

Castor et Pollux (Ballet Suite)
The Baroque Chamber Orchestra, Marcel Bernard, cond.
Baroque BU-2825

Concerto No. 6 in G Minor: Mvt. II
Moscow Chamber Orchestra, Rudolf Barshai, cond.
Monitor 2018

Concerto en sextour: No. 6   L'Enharmonique
Toulouse Chamber Orchestra, Louis Auriacombe, cond.
Music Guild M-4   stereo (s) 103

Concerto en sextour: No. 2   'Le Boucon''
                       No. 5   ''La Cupis,'' ''Le Marais''
Hewitt Chamber Orchestra, Maurice Hewitt, cond.
Haydn Society HSL-99

Indes Galantes (Suite):   Rigaudons I and II
                          Air Pour Zéphyre
                          Musette en roundeau
                          Air pour les Fleurs
Orchestre de Cahmbre des Concerts Lamoureux,
     Louis de Froment, cond.
Oiseau Lyre OL-50194   stereo 60024

La Princesse de Navarre (Suite)   Mvts. II, IV, V
The Baroque Chamber Ensemble
Baroque 1803

Les Paladins: Entree tres gaye Troubadours
                Sarabande
                Gaiment
                Menuet en rondeau
Orchestre des Concerts Lamoureux, Pierre Colombo, cond.
Oiseau Lyre OL-50106

Suite of Dances: Sommeio (Dardanus)
                   Minuets I and II (Platee)
                   Gavottes I and II (Zephyre)
                   Sarabande (Zais)
Orchestre de Chambre des Concerts Lamoureux,
     Louis de Froment, cond.
Oiseau Lyre OL-50194   stereo 60024

RANGSTROM, TRUE (1884-1947)

Divertimento Elegiaco for String Orchestra: Mvts. I, II
Royal Swedish Orchestra, Stig Westerberg, cond.
Westminster 18131

RASSE, FRANCOIS (1873-1955)

Concerto for Violin in C Major: Mvt. II
Robert Hosselet, violin
Belgian National Orchestra, Defossez, cond.
London International W-91063

RAVEL, MAURICE (1875-1937)

Daphnis and Chloe: Nocturne
Boston Symphony Orchestra, Charles Munch, cond.
Victor LSC-2568

Mother Goose Suite: Pavane of the Sleeping Beauty
                      Petit Poucet
French National Radio Orchestra, André Cluytens, cond.
Angel 35173

RAVEL, MAURICE (Cont.)

Pavane pour une infante défunte (1899)
Minneapolis Symphony Orchestra, Antal Dorati, cond.
Mercury MG-50005 stereo 18029

Quartet for Strings in F Major: Mvts. II
Juilliard String Quartet
Victor LM-2413 stereo LSC-2413

RAWSTHORNE, ALAN (1905-   )

Divertimento for Chamber Music: Lullaby: Mvt. II
Northern Sinfonia Orchestra, Boris Brott, cond.
Mace MCS 9068

REFICE, LICINIO (1885-1954)

La Samaritana: Preludio
Trittico Francesano: Le Stimmati
Scarlatti Orchestra of Naples, Refice, cond.
Colosseum 1043

REGER, MAX (1873-1916)

Ballet Suite, Opus 130: Columbine; Pierrot and Pierrette
Dresden Philharmonic Orchestra, Ernst Schrader, cond.
Urania 7050

Bocklin Suite, Opus 128: The Fiddling Hermit
German Philharmonic of Prague, Joseph Keilberth, cond.
Capitol P-8011

Chorale Preludes for Organ, Opus 67:
No. 1 — He Who Suffers God To Guide Him
No. 2 — O Sacred Head, Now Wounded
No. 4 — God of Heaven and Earth
No. 7 — Bridegroom Of My Soul
Ludwig Altman, organ
Music Library 7054

Serenade for Orchestra, Opus 95: Mvt. III
Amsterdam Concertgebouw, Eugen Jochum, cond.
Capitol P-8026

REICHEL, BERNARD (1901-   )

Suite Symphonique (1955): Mvt. I
Louisville Orchestra, Robert Whitney, cond.
Louisville LOU-575

RESPIGHI, OTTORINO (1879-1936)

Ancient Airs and Dances for the Lute:
Galiarda
Suite No. 1: Villanella
Suite No. 2: Campanae Parisienses
Suite No. 3: Arie di Corte
Philharmonia Hungarica, Antal Dorati, cond.
Mercury MG-50199 stereo 90199

The Birds: Mvt. II — The Dove
Mvt. IV. — The Nightingale
Vienna State Opera Orchestra, Franz Litschauer, cond.
Vanguard 433

The Birds: Mvt. II — The Dove
Scarlatti Orchestra of Naples, Caracciolo, cond.
Angel 35310

Brazilian Impressions: Tropical Night
Philharmonia Orchestra, Aleco Galliera, cond.
Angel 35405

RESPIGHI, OTTORINO (Cont.)

Church Windows: No. 3 — The Matins of Santa Chiara
Minneapolis Symphony Orchestra, Anatal Dorati, cond.
Mercury MG-50046

The Fountains of Rome: No. 1 — The Fountain of the Villa Giulia
No. 4 — The Villa Medici Fountain at Sunset
Philharmonia Orchestra, Aleco Galliere, cond.
Angel 35405

The Pines of Rome: The Pines of the Gianicolo
NBC Symphony Orchestra, Arturo Toscanini, cond.
Victor LM-1768

RHEINBERGER, JOSEF (1839-1901)

Sonata No. 7 for Organ in F Minor, Opus 127: Mvt. II
E. Power Biggs, organ
Columbia ML-5199

RICCIOTTI, CARLO (1681-1756)

Concertino No. 2 in G Major: Mvt. II
Stuttgart Chamber Orchestra, Karl Munchinger, cond.
London CM-9275 stereo 6206

RICHTER, FRANZ X. (1709-1789)

Sinfonia con fuga in G Minor: Mvt. II
Spielgemeinschaft der Archive-Production
Archive 3159

Sinfonia in G Major: Mvt. II
Northern Sinfonia Orchestra, Boris Brott, cond.
Mace MCS 9069

RICHTER, MARGA (1926-   )

Aria and Toccata for Viola and String Orchestra: Aria
Walter Trampler, viola
MGM String Orchestra, Carlos Surinach, cond.
MGM 3559

RIEGGER, WALLINGFORD (1885-1961)

Romanza
Saint Cecelia Academy Orchestra, Alfredo Antonini
Composers Recordings, Inc. CRI-117

RIETI, VITTORIO (1898-   )

Madrigale: Mvt. II
MGM Chamber Orchestra, Arthur Winograd, cond.
MGM E-3414

Dance Variations: Theme
Chanconne (in part)
MGM String Orchestra, Carlos Surinach, cond.
MGM E-3365

RIISAGER, KNUDAGE (1897-   )

Concertino for Trumpet and Strings: Mvt. II
George Eskdale, trumpet
Danish State Radio Orchestra, Thomas Jensen, cond.
Mercury MG 15041

Fools' Paradise (ballet suite): Princess Sweets
Copenhagen Philharmonic, Thomas Jensen, cond.
His Master's Voice Z-250/1 (78 rpm)

RIMSKY-KORSAKOV, NIKOLAI (1844-1908)

Ivan The Terrible (suite): Intermezzo
London Symphony Orchestra, Anatole Fistoulari, cond.
MGM E-3076

RIVIER, JEAN (1896-   )

Symphony No. 2 for Strings: Adagio
MGM String Orchestra, Izler Solomon
MGM 3104

Symphony No. 3 for Strings in G Major: Mvt. III
French National Radio Orchestra, Georges Tzipine, cond.
Pathe DTX-286

ROGERS, BERNARD (1893-1968)

Five Fairy Tales: The Song of Rapunzel
Eastman-Rochester Orchestra, Howard Hanson, cond.
Mercury MG-50147   stereo 90147

Soliloguy for Flute and Strings
Joseph Mariano, flute
Eastman-Rochester Orchestra, Howard Hanson, cond.
Mercury MG-50076

ROMAN, JOHANN HELMICH (1694-1758)

Drottningholmsmusik: Mvts. II, III, IV
Camarata Lutetiensis, Eustache, flute
Nonesuch HC-73014

ROPARTZ, J. GUY (1864-1955)

Prelude, Marine and Chamson for Flute, Viola, Cello and Harp:
Nos. 1 and 2
The Melos Ensemble
Oiseau 50217   stereo 60048

ROREM, NED (1923-   )

Design for Orchestra (1955) (in part)
The Louisville Orchestra, Roberty Whitney, cond.
LOU 57-5

ROSENMULLER, JOHANN (1619-1684)

Sonata No. 2 in E Minor (entire)
Claude Monteus, flute; Harry Shulman, oboe
Bernard Greenhouse, cello; Sylvia Marlowe, harpsichord
Esoteric 517

ROSETTI, FRANCESCO ANTONIO (1746-1792)

Concerto for Horn in D Minor: Slow Movement
Erich Penzel, horn
Württemberg Chamber Orchestra, Jörg Faerber, cond.
Turnabout TV-4078

Concerto for Horn in E Flat Major: Mvt. III
Pasqualino Rossi, horn
Italian Chamber Orchestra, Newell Jenkins, cond.
Haydn Society 9034

ROSSINI, GIOACCHINO (1782-1868)

Quartets for Winds: Nos. 1, 4, 5, and 6
New York Woodwind Quartet
Samuel Baron, flute; David Glazer, clarinet;
Bernard Garfield, bassoon; John Barrows, horn
Dover 5214

ROSSINI-RESPIGHI

"La Boutique Fantasque": Valse lente, Nocturne
London Philharmonic, René Leibowitz, cond.
Parliament (1) 176

ROSSLER-ROSETTI
Notturno in D for Flute, Strings, Two Horns: Romance
Musici Pragenses
Crosswords 22 16 0066

ROUSSEL, ALBERT (1869-1937)
Bacchus and Ariane, Suite No. 2: Prelude
Boston Symphony Orchestra, Charles Munch, cond.
Victor LM-6113

Concerto for Small Orchestra, Opus 34: Mvt. II
Lamoureux Orchestra, Paul Sacher, cond.
Epic LC-3129

Petit Suite, Opus 39: Pastorale
Lamoureux Orchestra, Paul Sacher, cond.
Epic LC-3129

Quartet for Strings in D Major, Opus 45: Mvt. II
Loewenguth Quartet
Decca 4026

The Sandman
Paris Philharmonic, René Leibowitz, cond.
Esoteric 511

Serenade, Opus 30: Mvt. II
Pierre Jamet Instrumental Quintet
French HMV DB-11124/5 (78 rpm)

Trio for Flute, Viola and Cello, Opus 40: Mvt. II
Julius Baker, flute; Lillian Fuchs, viola
Harry Fuchs, cello
Decca 9777

ROZSA, MIKLOS (1907-   )
Concerto for Violin and Orchestra: Mvt. II
Jascha Heifetz, violin
Dallas Symphony Orchestra, Walter Hendl, cond.
Victor LM-2027

Theme and Variations for Violin, Cello and Orchestra
Parts: 1, 2 and 6
Jascha Heifetz, violin; Gregor Piatigorsky, cello;
Chamber orchestra
Victor LM-2770

RUBBRA, EDMUND (1901-   )
Improvisations on Virginal Pieces, Opus 50: "Loth to Depart"
The Halle Orchestra, Sir John Barbirolli, cond.
His Master's Voice DB-9715 (78 rpm)

Quartet No. 2 for Strings in E Flat: Mvts. II, III
The Griller String Quartet
London LL-1550

Symphony No. 5 in B Flat Major: Mvt. III
The Halle Orchestra, Sir John Barbirolli, cond.
His Master's Voice LHMV-1011

RUGGIERI, GIOVANNI BATISTA (XVII Century)
Sonata in G Minor, Opus 3, No. 5 (omit final allegro)
Musica Sacra AMS-46

Trio Sonata in G Major, Opus 3, No. 8: Mvt. III
Societas Musica of Copenhagen, Jorgen Ernst Hansen, cond.
Haydn Society 9057

RUST, FRIEDRICH WILLIAM (1739-1796)
Sonata for Viola, Two Horns and Cello: Mvt. II
Joseph de Pasquale, viola
Samuel Mayes, cello
James Stagliano, Harry Shapiro, horns
Boston Records B-201

SACHSEN-WEIMAR
Concerto in B Major: Slow movement
Concerto in C Major: Slow movement
International Solosit Orchestra, Koppenburg, cond.
Mace 9021

SAINT-SAENS, CAMILLE (1835-1921)
Concerto No. 3 for Violin in B Minor, Opus 61: Andantino
Zino Francescatti, violin
New York Philharmonic, Dimitri Mitropoulos, cond.
Columbia ML-4315 stereo MS 6268

Havanaise for Violin and Orchestra (in part)
Aaron Rosand, violin
Southwest German Radio Orchestra, Rolf Reinhardt, cond.
VOX PL-10470

Suite Algerienne, Opus 60: Mvt. III
Frankenland State Symphony of Nuremberg, George Barati, cond.
Lyrichord LL-103

Symphony No. 2 in A Minor, Opus 55: Mvt. II
Netherlands Philharmonic, Walter Goehr, cond.
Concert Hall Society 1180

SALIERI, ANTONIO (1750-1825)
Concerto in C Major for Flute, Oboe and Orchestra: Mvt. II
Andre Lardrot, flute; Raymond Meyland, oboe;
I Solisti de Zagreb, Janigro, cond.
Vanguard VRS-1133 stereo 71133

SAMMARTINI, GIOVANNI BATTISTA (1701-1775)
Concerto No. 2 for Violin in C Major: Mvt. II
Antonio Abussi, violin
Italian Chamber Orchestra, Newell Jenkins, cond.
Haydn Society 9034

Symphony in A Major: Mvt. II
Symphony in G Major: Mvt. II
Symphony in A for Two Horns and Strings: Mvt. II
Orchestre Accademia dell'Orso, Newell Jenkins, cond.
Period 731

SAMMARTINI, GIUSEPPE (c.1693-c.1750)
Concerto in F Major for Flute: Mvt. II
Jean-Pierre Rampal, flute
Saar Chamber Orchestra, Karl Ristenpart, cond.
Epic BC-1293

Concerto for Oboe and Orchestra in F Major: Mvt. III
Sidney Gallesi, oboe
Italian Chamber Orchestra, Newell Jenkins, cond.
Haydn Society 9027

SANDERS, ROBERT L. (1906-   )
Little Symphony No. 2 in B Flat Major: Mvt. II
The Louisville Orchestra, Robert Whitney, cond.
Louisville LOU-5457

SANTA-CRUZ, DOMINGO (1899-   )

Sinfonia No. 2, Opus 25: Mvts. I, III
MGM String Orchestra, Carlos Surinach, cond.
MGM E-3444

SARRO, DOMENICO (1679-1744)

Sonata in A Minor for Flute, Strings & Harpsichord: Mvts. I, II
Meylan, flute
Saar Chamber Orchestra, Karl Ristenpart, cond.
Odessey 32 16 0015   stereo 32 16 0016

SATIE, ERIK (1866-1925)

Trios Gymnopedies (1888)
Concert Arts Orchestra, Vladimir Golschmann, cond.
Capitol P-8244

SCARLATTI, ALESSANDRO (1659-1725)

Concerto No. 3 in F Major: Mvts. II, IV
Scarlatti Orchestra of Naples, Franco Caracciolo, cond.
Angel 35141

Concerto No. 6 in F Major for Strings: Mvts. II, IV
Virtuosi di Roma, Renato Fasano, cond.
Decca 9572

Quintet in F Major: Mvt. I
Ensemble Baroque de Paris
Boite a Musique LD-011

Sinfonia No. 5 in D Minor: Mvts. I, III
Scarlatti Orchestra of Naples, Franco Caracciolo, cond.
Angel 35141

Sonata a Quattro in D Minor: Mvt. II
New Music String Quartet
Bartok 911

Sonata for Flute and Strings (arr. Tailleferre): Mvt. III
Instrumental Quintet of Paris
Victor 4250/1 (78rpm)

Sonata for String Orchestra
Allegro Chamber Orchestra, Jan Tubbs, cond.
Allegro 3146

SCARLATTI, DOMENICO (1685-1757)

Concerto in G Major for Oboe (arr. Bryan): Mvts. III, IV
Leon Goossens, oboe
Philharmonia String Orchestra, Walter Süsskind, cond.
English Columbia DX-8347/8 (78 rpm)

SCARLATTI-TOMMASINI

The Good Humored Ladies (ballet suite): Mvt. III
Vienna State Opera Orchestra, Franz Litschauer
Vanguard 440

SCHEIDT, SAMUEL (1587-1634)

Christmas Chorales
Frederick Högner, Steinmeyer Organ at Munich
Cantate 642 212

Da Jesus an dem Kreuze Stund
Robert Noehren, Organ of Kenmore Presbyterian Church,
Buffalo, New York
Allegro LEG-9016

Pavan in A Minor
Leonhardt Consort
Telefunken AWT-9461

102

SCHILDT, MELCHIOR (1593-1667)

Chorale Variations: "Heer Christ der einig Gottes Sohn"
J. Ernst Hansen, organ
Nonesuch H-1110

SCHLICK, ARNOLT (c.1460—after 1517)

Maria Zart on Eler Art
Robert Noehren, Organ of Kenmore Presbyterian Church,
Buffalo, New York
Allegro LEG-9016

SCHMIDT, FRANZ (1874-1939)

Symphony No. 4 in C Major: Mvts. I, II, IV
Vienna Symphony Orchestra, Rudolf Moralt, cond.
Epic LC-3164

SCHOECK, OTHMAR (1886-1957)

Concerto Opus 65 for Horn and String Orchestra: Mvt. II
Josef Breuza, horn
Zurich Orchestra, Edmond de Stoutz, cond.
Mace MCS 9047

SCHONBERG, ARNOLD (1874-1951)

Five Pieces for Orchestra, Opus 16: "Summer Morning by a Lake"
"Yesteryears"
Chicago Symphony Orchestra, Rafael Kubelik, cond.
Mercury MG-50024

SCHUBERT, FRANZ (1797-1828)

Concerto in A Minor for Cello ("Arpeggione"): Mvt. II
Gaspar Cassado, cello (arr. Cassado
Bamberg Symphony, Jonel Perlea, cond.
Vox PL-10-210

Hirtenlied (from "Rosamunde")
Philadelphia Woodwind Quintet
Columbia ML-5984

Litany for the Feast of All Soul's Day
E. Power Biggs, organ
Columbia ML-4603

Minuets and German Dances (1813)
Minuet No. 3 in D Major
Minuet No. 5 in C Major (Trio)
Dance No. 1 in C Major (Trio)
Dance No. 2 in G Major (Trio)
Stuttgart Chamber Orchestra, Münchinger, cond.
London LL-1393 stereo STS-15035

Octet in F Major for Strings and Winds, Opus 166: Mvt. II
Wlach, Oehlberger, Von Freiberg, Hermann
Vienna Konzerthaus Quartet
Westminster 9044

Quartet for Flute , Guitar, Viola and Cello in G Major: Mvt. III
Mess, Faiss, Kirchner, S. Barchet
Period 730

Quartet No. 1 for Strings in B Flat Major: Mvt. II
Endres String Quartet
Vox VBX-5

Quartet No. 6 for Strings in D Major: Mvt. II
Endres String Quartet
Vox VBX-5

SCHUBERT, FRANZ (Cont.)

Quartet No. 10 in E Flat Major, Opus 125, No. 1: Mvt. III
Vienna Konzerthaus Quartet
Westminster 18476

Quartet No. 13 in A Minor, Opus 29: Mvt. II
Budapest String Quartet
Columbia ML-4831

Symphony No. 2 in B Flat Major: Mvt. II
Stuttgart Philharmonic Orchestra, W. Van Hoogstraten, cond.
Period SPLP-517

Symphony No. 3 in D Major: Mvt. II
Stuttgart Philharmonic Orchestra, W. Van Hoogstraten, cond.
Period SPLP-517

Symphony No. 5 in B Flat Major: Mvt. II
Royal Philharmonic Orchestra, Sir. Thomas Beecham, cond.
Capitol G-7212   stereo SG-7212

Symphony No. 7 in E Major: (Arr. Weingartner): Mvt. II
Vienna State Opera Orchestra, Franz Litschauer, cond.
Vanguard VRS-427

SCHUMAN, WILLIAM (1910-   )

A Song of Orpheus (in part)
Leonard Rose, cello
Cleveland Orchestra, George Szell, cond.
Columbia ML-6038   MS-6638

Credendum: (excerpts)
The Philadelphia Orchestra, Eugene Ormandy, cond.
Columbia ML-5185

Symphony for Strings: Mvt. II
Pittsburg Symphony, William Steinberg, cond.
Capitol S-8212

Symphony No. 3: Chorale
New York Philharmonic, Leonard Bernstein, cond.
Columbia ML-5645   stereo MS-6245

Symphony No. 6: Adagio (in part)
The Philadelphia Orchestra, Eugene Ormandy, cond.
Columbia ML-4992

SCHUMANN, ROBERT (1810-1856)

Concerto for Cello in A Minor, Opus 129: Langsam
Pablo Casals, cello
Prades Festival Orchestra
Columbia ML-4926

Concerto for Four Horns, Opus 86: Mvt. I
USSR State Radio Orchestra, Alexander Gauk, cond.
Monitor 2023

Symphony No. 2 in C Major, Opus 61: Mvt. II
Israel Philharmonic, Paul Kletski, cond.
Angel 35373

Symphony No. 3 in E Flat, Opus 97 ("Rhenish"): Mvt. III
New York Philharmonic, Leonard Bernstein, cond.
Columbia ML-5694   stereo MS-6294

SCIANNI, JOSEPH (1928-   )

Adagio Cantabile
Eastman-Rochester Orchestra, Howard Hanson, cond.
Mercury MG-50053*   stereo 90053*

_____

*Music for Quet Listening album.

SCOTT, TOM (1912-   )

Binorie Variations
> Vienna Symphony Orchestra, F. Charles Adler, cond.
> Composers Recordings, Inc. CRI-104

SEROCKI, KAZIMIERZ (1922-   )

Sinfonietta for Two String Orchestras (19560: Mvt. II
> Warsaw National Philharmonic, Witold Rowicki, cond.
> Phillips PHS 900-141   stereo 900141

SESSIONS, ROGER (1896-   )

Symphony No. 1 (19270: Mvt. II
> Japan Philharmonic, Akeo Watanabe, cond.
> Composers Recordings, Inc. CRI-131

SHOSTAKOVICH, DMITRI (1906-   )

Ballet Suite No. 1: Mvts. III (in part), IV
Ballet Suite No. 3: Mvt. III
> State Radio Orchestra of the USSR
> Alexander Gauk and Abram Stassevich, conductors
> Classic Editions 3012

Concerto for Violin and Orchestra, Opus 99: Mvt. I
> David Oistrakh, violin
> New York Philharmonic, Dimitri Mitropoulos, cond.
> Columbia ML-5077

Quartet No. 1 for Strings: Mvts. I, II
> Guilet String Quartet
> MGM E-3113

Quartet No. 4 for Strings: Mvt. II
> Borodin String Quartet
> Mercury MG-50309

Quartet No. 7 for Strings: (in part)
> The Beethoven Quartet
> Baroque 1864

Quartet No. 8 for Strings: (in part)
> Borodin String Quartet
> Mercury MG-50309

Symphony No. 5, Opus 47: Mvt. III
> New York Stadium Orchestra, Leopold Stokowski, cond.
> Everest 6010   stereo 3010

Symphony No. 6, Opus 54: Mvt. I
> London Philharmonic Orchestra, Sir Adrian Boult, cond.
> Everest 6007

Symphony No. 9, Opus 70: Mvt. II
> London Symphony Orchestra, Sir Malcolm Sargent
> Everest 6054   stereo 3054

SIBELIUS, JAN (1865-1957)

Bard, Opus 64   (1913)
> Philharmonic Promenade Orchestra, Sir Adrian Boult, cond.
> Vanguard 489

Belshazzar's Feast, Opus 51 (1906)
>> No. 2 — "Solitude"
>> No. 3 — "Night Music"
> London Symphony Orchestra, Kajanus, cond.
> Victor M-715   (78 rpm)

Cansonetta, Opus 62a
> The Arthur Winograd String Ensemble
> MGM E-3335

105

SIBELIUS, JAN (Cont.)

Humoresque for Violin and Orchestra, Opus 89, No. 2 (1917)
Aaron Rosand, violin
Southwest German Radio Orchestra, Tibor Szőke, cond.
VOX STPL 511.600

King Christian II Suite, Opus 27: Elegy
Birmingham Orchestra, George Weldon, cond.
English Columbia DX-1220 (78 rpm)

Lemminkainen Suite, Opus 22: No. 3 — "Swan of Tuonela"
Philadelphia Orchestra, Eugene Ormandy, cond.
Columbia ML-5181

Pélleas et Melisande Suite: "Mélisande"
"The Blind Sisters"
"Pastorale"
"Death of Mélisande"
Royal Philharmonic, Sir Thomas Beecham, cond.
Columbia ML-4550

Quartet in D Minor for Strings, Opus 56: Mvt. III
Copenhagen String Quartet
Turnabout TV (3) 4091

Rakastava, Opus 14 (1911): "The Lover"
"The Way of The Lover"
"Good Evening, My Love!" "Farewell"
The Arthur Winograd String Ensemble
MGM E-3335

Romance in C Major for Strings, Opus 42 (1903)
Cleveland Sinfonietta, Louis Lane, cond.
Epic BC-1275

Scènes Historiques, Opus 66: "Love Song"
Royal Philharmonic, Sir Thomas Beecham, cond.
Columbia ML-4550

Symphony No. 4 in A Minor, Opus 63, (1911): Mvt. III
Philharmonia Orchestra, Herbert Von Karajan, cond.
Angel 35082

Symphony No. 7 in C Major, Opus 105, (1924)
Royal Philharmonic, Sir Thomas Beecham, cond.
Angel 35458

The Tempest Suite, Opus 109: "Berceuse"
"Chorus of the Winds"
Stockholm Radio Orchestra, Stig Westerberg, cond.
Westminster 18529

SMETANA, BEDRICH (1824-1888)

From Bohemia's Meadows and Forests (in part)
The High Castle (in part)
The Chicago Symphony Orchestra, Rafael Kubelik, cond.
Mercury SRW-18026

Quartet No. 1 for Strings in E Minor: Mvt. III
Koeckert String Quartet
Decca 9637

SMITH, JOHN CHRISTOPHER (1712-1795)

Minature Suite (arr. McDonald): Air
Arthur Fiedler Sinfonietta
Victor M-609 (78 rpm)

SOMMER, JOHANN (unknown)

Pavan
Concentus Musicus
Bach Guild BG-626

106

SOWANDE, FELA

African Suite for Strings: Onipe-Lullaby
New Symphony Orchestra, Harvey, cond.
London LPS-426

SOWERBY, LEO (1895-1968)

Ballade for Viola and Organ
Paul Doktor, viola
Marilyn Mason, organ
Mirrosonic 1013

From the Northland: "Burnt Rock Pool"
Dean Dixon and Orchestra
American Recording Society 14

SPOHR,LUDWIG (1784-1859)

Concerto for Clarinet in F Minor: Mvt. II
Franz Hammerle, clarinet
Linz Bruckner Symphony, Georg Ludwig Jochum, cond.
Urania 7021

Concerto No. 7 for Violin in E Minor: Mvt. II
Rudolf Schulz, violin
Berlin Radio Symphony, Robert Heger, cond.
Urania 7049

Duos Concertants for Two Violins; No. 2 in D Minor: Mvt. I
David and Igor Oistrakh, violins
Monitor MC-2085

Nonet in F Major, Opus 31: Mvt. III
New York Woodwind Quintet
Fine Arts Quartet
Concert Disc 1201   stereo 201

STAMIC, JAN VACLAV (1717-1757) (better known as Johann Stamitz)

Symphony in A Major, ("Spring"): Mvt. II
Prague Chamber Orchestra, Otakar Trhlik, cond.
Supraphone MAB-2

STAMITZ, JOHANN WENZEL ANTON (1717-1757)

Concerto for Clarinet in B Flat Major: Mvt. II
Jost Michaels, clarinet
Munich Chamber Orchestra, Carl Gorvin, cond.
Archive 3092

Sinfonie in D Major: Mvt. II
Munich Chamber Orchestra, Carl Gorvin, cond.
Archive 3092

STAMITZ, KARL (1745-1801)

Concerto for Flute and Orchestra in D Major: Mvt. II
Concerto for Flute and Orchestra in G Major: Mvt. II
Kurt Redel, flute
Oiseau-Lyre Orchestral Ensemble
Oiseau-Lyre OL-50035

Concerto for Viola in D Major: Mvt. II
Heinz Wigand, viola
Stuttgart Pro Musica, Rolf Reinhardt, cond.
VOX PL-10720

Quartet in E Flat Major, Opus 8, No. 2: Mvt. II
Vienna Wind Quintet
Music Guild M-28   stereo (s) 110

Quartet for Orchestra, Opus 4, No. 4 in F Major: Mvt. II
Spielgemeinschaft der Archive-Production
Wolfgang Hofmann, cond.
Archive 3159

STAMITZ, KARL (Cont.)

Seven Serenades from Opus 28
   The Eichendorff Wind Group
   Musical Heritage 524

Symphony Concertante for Two Violins and Orchestra: Mvt. II
   Helmut Winschermann, solo oboe
   Saar Chamber Orchestra, Ristenpart, cond.
   Nonesuch H-1014   stereo 71014

STEHMAN, JACQUES (1912-   )

Symphonie de Poche: Mvt. III
   Belgian National Orchestra, Edouard Van Remoortel
   London International 91082

STERN, ROBERT (1934-   )

In Memoriam Abraham
   Eastman-Rochester Orchestra, Howard Hanson, cond.
   Mercury MG-50053*   stereo 90053*

STEVENS, HALSEY (1908-   )

Sinfonia Breve: Mvt. II
   The Louisville Orchestra, Robert Whitney, cond.
   Louisville LOU-593

Triskelion: Mvt. II
   The Louisville Orchestra, Robert Whitney, cond.
   Louisville LOU-545-1

STOELZEL, GOTTFRIED HEINRICH (1690-1749)

Concerto for Two Orchestras: Mvts. I, III
   Dresden Chamber Soloists, Marcel Bernard
   Baroque BU-1820

Trio Sonata in C Minor: Mvts. I, III
   Eichendorf Wind Group
   Musical Heritage MHS-581

STOUT, LOUIS (arranger)

The Cuckoo
   Chicago Horn Quartet
   Concert Disc M-1243

STRADELLA, ALESSANDRO (1642-1682)

Arai di Chiesa
   Societa Corelli
   RCA Italiana LM-20004

STRAUSS, RICHARD (1864-1949)

Aus Italien, Symphonic Fantasy, Opus 16, (1886): "On The Shores
      of Sorrento"
   Vienna Philharmonic, Clemens Krauss, cond.
   London LL-969

Le Bourgeois Gentilhomme, Suite: Opus 60, (1916):
      1. Overture (allegretto only)
      2. Minuet
      5. Lully's Minuet
      7. Entry of Cleonte (in part)
   Philharmonia Orchestra, Wolfgang Sawallisch, cond.
   Angel 35646

Concerto No. 1 for Horn in E Flat Major (1884): Mvt. II
Concerto No. 2 for Horn in E Flat Major (1942): Mvt. II
   Dennis Brain, horn
   Angel 35496

----

*Music for Quet Listening album.

STRAUSS, RICHARD (Cont.)

Dance Suite after Couperin (1923): Mvts. IV, VI
    Frankenland State Symphony, Erich Kloss, cond.
    Lyrichord LL-58

Divertimento after Couperin, Opus 86 (1941):
        La Visionaire
        Musette de Choisy
        La fin Madelon
        La Douce Janneton
        La Sëzile
        Musette de Taverny
        Las fauvettes plaintives
        Le Tours de Passe-passe
        Les Ombres errantes
        L'Anguille
        Les jeunes Seigneurs
        La Linotte effarouchée
    Bamberger Symphony, Clemens Krauss, cond.
    Amadeo AVRS 5033

Metamorphosen (1944-54)
    French National Radio Orchestra, Jascha Horenstein, cond.
    Angel 35101

Serenade for 13 Winds in E Flat Major, Opus 7 (1881)
    Eastman Wind Ensemble, Frederick Fennell, cond.
    Mercury MG-50173 stereo 90173

Suite for Winds in B Flat Major, Opus 4: Romanza
    Vienna Philharmonic Wind Group
    Westminster 18173

Symphonia Domestica, Opus 53, (1904): Cradel Song
    Chicago Symphony Orchestra, Fritz Reiner, cond.
    Victor LM-2103

Symphony for Wind Instruments in E Flat Major: Mvt. II
    MGM Orchestra, Izler Solomon, cond.
    MGM E-3097

Zwischenspiel aus "Capriccio"
    Bavarian Radio Orchestra, Clemens Krauss , cond.
    Amadeo AVRS 5033

STRAVINSKY, IGOR (1882-   )

Apollo Ballet (Apollon Musagete) (1928): In Part
Orpheus Ballet (19480: In Part
    Columbia Symphony Orchestra, Stravinsky, cond.
    Columbia ML-6046   Stereo MS-6646

Etudes for Orchestra (1930): Cantique
    Orchestre National de la R.T.F., Pierre Boulez, cond.
    Nonesuch H-1093   stereo 71093

Norwegian Moons: No. 2 — "Song"
    Philharmonic Symphony of New York, Stravnisky, cond.
    Columbia ML-4398

Pastorale for Violin and Wind Instruments
    Philadelphia Woodwind Quintet
    Veda Reynolds, violin
    Louis Rosenblatt, English horn
    Columbia ML-5984

SUK, JOSEF (1874-1935)

Serenade for Strings in E Flat, Opus 6: Mvt. III
    Kapp Sinfonietta Strings, Emanuel Vardi, cond.
    Kapp 9054   stereo S-9054

SUK, JOSEF (Cont.)

Symphony No. 2 in C Minor ("Asrael"): Mvts. II, IV, V (in part)
Czech Philharmonic, Vaclav Talich, cond.
Artia 107

SUTCLIFFE, JAMES (1929-   )

Gymnopédie
Eastman-Rochester Orchestra, Howard Hanson, cond.
Mercury MG-50053* stereo 90053*

SZYMANOWSKI, KAROL (1882-1937)

Quartet No. 1 in C Major, Opus 37 (1917): Mvt. II
The Walden String Quartet
Lyrichord LL-22

TANEYEV, SERGEY (1856-1915)

Suite de Concert, Opus 28: Mvt. IV (in part)
David Oistrakh, violin
Philharmonia Orchestra, Nicolai Malko, cond.
Angel 35355

Trio in D Major, Opus 21: Mvt. III
David Oistrakh, Peter Bondarenko, violins
Mikhael Terian, viola
Monitor 2059

TANSMAN, ALEXANDRE (1897-   )

Capricco (1955): Nocturne
The Louisville Orchestra, Robert Whitney, cond.
Louisville LOU 5-62

Isaiah The Prophet: Interlude II
Radio Philharmonic Orchestra, Paul Van Kempen, cond.
Epic LC-3289

TARTINI, GIUSEPPE (1692-1770)

Andante in D Major
Paul Doktor, viola; Marilyn Mason, organ
Mirrosonic RM-1013

Concerto in A Major for Cello and Strings: Mvt. II
Enrico Mainardi, cello
Lucerne Festival Strings, Wolfgang Schneiderhan, cond.
Archive 3117

Concerto in D Major for Cello: Mvts. I, III
Concerto in G Minor for Cello: Mvts. I, III
Vera Dénes, cello
Hungarian Chamber Orchestra, Wilmos Tátrai, cond.
Monitor MC-2056 stereo S-2056

Concerto in G Major for Flute: Mvt. II
Jean-Pierre Rampal, flute
Saar Chamber Orchestra, Karl Ristenpart, cond.
Epic BC-1293

Concerto Grosso in A Minor: Mvt. II
Angelicum Orchestra of Milan, Claudio Abbado, cond.
Music Guild M-33

―――――――
*Music for Quet Listening Album.

TARTINI, GIUSEPPE (Cont.)

Concerti for Violin and Strings, Opus 2:
  No. 2 in C Major: Mvt. II
  No. 3 in B Minor: Mvt. II
  No. 4 in F Major: Mvt. II
  No. 5 in C Major: Mvt. II
  No. 6 in E Major: Mvt. II
 Renato Biffoli, violin
 I Musici, Dean Eckertsen, cond.
 Vox DL-373

Concerto in D Minor for Violin: Mvt. II
 Wolfgang Schneiderhan, violin
 Lucerne Festival Strings
 Archive 3117

Concerto in D Major for Violin: Mvt. II
Concerto in F Major for Violin: Mvt. II
 Franco Gulli, violin
 Angelicum Orchestra of Milan, Claudio Abbado, cond.
 Music Guild M-33

Concerto in E Major for Violin: Mvt. II
 Ferro, violin
 Virtuosi di Roma, Renato Fasano, cond.
 Decca 9572

Concerto in F Major for Violin: Mvt. II
 Wolfgang Schneiderhan, violin
 Vienna Orchestra, F. Charles Adler, cond.
 SPA-46

Concerto for Violin in G Minor: Mvt. II
 Rostal, Winterthur Symphony; Walter Goehr, cond.
 Concert Hall Society 1174

Concerto No. 58 in F Major: Mvt. II
 Scarlatti Orchestra of Naples, Franco Caracciolo, cond.
 Angel 35255

Sinfonia in A Major: Mvt. II
 London Baroque Ensemble, Karl Haas, cond.
 Decca 4081

Sinfonia in D Major: Mvt. II
 Lucerne Festival Strings, Wolfgang Schneiderhan, cond.
 Archive 3117

Sinfonia Pastorale for Violin and Strings: Mvt. III
 Jan Tomasow, violin solo
 Vienna State Opera Chamber Orchestra
 Vanguard S-154

Sonata a Quattro in D Major: Mvt. II
 New Music String Quartet
 Bartok 911

Trio Sonata in F Major for Two Violins: Mvt. I
 David and Igor Oistrakh, violins
 Helidor HS-25009

Trio Sonata in F Major for Two Violins: Mvt. I
 David and Igor Oistrakh, violins
 Decca DL-9950

TAVERNER, JOHN (c.1495-1545)

In Nominee
 The In Nominee Players
 Vanguard-Bach Guild BG-576

TCHAIKOVSKY, PETER I. (1840-1893)

Autumn Song, from "The Seasons," Opus 37A
Bolshoi Theatre Orchestra, Leopold Steinberg, cond.
Colosseum 137

Serenade Melancolique for Violin, Opus 26
Aaron Rosand, violin
Southwest German Radio Orchestra, Tibor Szőke, cond.
VOX (5) 11600

Souvenir of Florence, Opus 70: Mvt. II
Leonid Kogan, Elizaveta Gilels, violins
Rudloph Barshai, Heinrich Talalian, violas
Sviatoslav Knushevitzky, Mstislav Rostropovich, cellos
Monitor MC-2019

Suite No. 4 for Orchestra in G Major, Opus 61 ("Mozartiana"): Mvt. III
Lamoureux Orchestra, Paul Van Kempen, cond.
Epic LC-3212

Symphony No. 1 in G Minor, Opus 13, ("Winter Dreams"): Adagio (in part)
Bolshoi Symphony Orchestra, Golovanov, cond.
Westminster XWN-18224

Symphony No. 7 in E Flat Major (arr. Bogatyryev): Mvt. II
The Philadelphia Orchestra, Eugene Ormandy, cond.
Columbia ML-5749   stereo MS-6349

Variations on a Rococo Theme for Cello, Opus 33: (in part)
Mstislav Rostropovich, cello
Moscow State Orchestra, Kiril Kondreshin, cond.
Period SHO-337

TELEMANN, GEORG PHILIPP (1681-1767)

Concerto for German Flute, Oboe d'Amore, Viola d'Amore,
Strings and Continuo in E Major:
Hans-Peter Schmitz, flute; Hermann Tottcher, Oboe d'Amore;
Kammermusikkreis Emil Seiler
Archive 3109

Concerto in A Minor for Two Flutes: Mvt. III
Austrian Tonkuenstler Orchestra, Kurt List, cond.
Musical Heritage Society MHS 743

Concerto in A Major for Flute, Violin and Strings: Mvt. III
Concerto Amsterdam, Franz Brüggen, cond.
Telefunken AWT 9449/50

Concerto in D Minor for Oboe and Strings: Mvt. I
Andre Lardrot, oboe
I Soloisti di Zagreb, Antonio Janigro, cond.
Bach Guild 575   stereo 5028

Concerto in F Minor for Oboe and Strings: Mvt. II
Harry Shulman, oboe
Orchestra conducted by Daniel Saidenberg
Kapp 9041   stereo 9041-S

Concerto in C Minor for Oboe: Mvt. III
Lothar Koch, oboe
Hamburg Telemann Society Orchestra, Wilifried Bottcher, cond.
Archive 3224

Concerto in E Minor for Oboe: Mvts. I, III
Kurt Kalmus, oboe
Munich Pro Arte, Jurt Redel, cond.
Westminster XWN-7540

TELEMANN, GEORG PHILIPP (Cont.)

Concerto in C Major for Oboe and Strings: Mvt. II
Concerto in C Major for Two Violins and Strings: Mvt. II
Concerto in D Major for Trumpet, Two Oboes and Strings: Mvt. II
     Saar Radio Chamber Orchestra, Karl Ristenpart, cond.
     Musical Heritage Soceity MHS-751

Concerto in D Minor for Oboe: Mvt. I
     Harold Gomberg, oboe
     Columbia Chamber Orchestra, Seiji Ozawa
     Columbia ML-6232

Concerto in A Major for Oboe d'Amore: Mvts. I, III
     Robert Casier, oboe d'amore
     Toulouse Chamber Orchestra, Louis Auriacombe, cond.
     Nonesuch H-1066 stereo 71066

Concerto in B Flat for Three Oboes, Three Violins and Basso
        Continuo: Mvt. II
     Moscow Chamber Orchestra, Barshai, cond.
     Angel 36264 stereo S-36264

Concerto in E Minor for Recorder, German Flute, Strings and
        Continuo: Mvt. IV
     Sparr Schaeffer, Meyer with Chamber Orchestra
     Archive 3109

Concerto in C Major for Recorder and Strings: Mvt. III
     Bernard Krainis, alto recorder
     The London Strings, Neville Marriner, cond.
     Mercury MG-50443

Concerto in D Major for Trumpet and Strings: Mvt. III
     Munich Pro Arte Chamber Orchestra, Kurt Redel, cond.
     Musical Heritage Society MHS-518

Concerto in D Major for Trumpet and Strings: Mvt. III
     Bach Orchestra of Hamburg, Robert Stehli, cond.
     Archive ARC-3119

Concerto in D Major for Trumpet, Two Violins and Continuo: Mvt. III
     Scherbaum, trumpet;
     Bach Orchestra of Hamburg, Robert Stehli, cond.
     Archive 3119

Concerto in D Major for Three Trumpets, Two Oboes and
        String Orchestra: Mvt. II
     The Paillard Chamber Orchestra
     Musical Heritage Society MHS-549

Concerto in G Major for Viola and Strings: Mvt. III
     Heinz Kirchner, viola
     Stuttgart Chamber Orchestra, Karl Münchinger, cond.
     London CM-9144

Concerto in A Minor for Violin and Strings: Mvt. II
     Jelka Krek, violin
     I Soloisti di Zagreb, Antonio Janigro, cond.
     Bach Guild 575

Concerto in G Major for Two Violins: Mvt. II
     Reytl, Steinhausler, violins;
     Pro Arte Chamber Orchestra of Munich, Kurt Redel, cond.
     Westminster XWN 19042 stereo 17042

Concerto in G Major for Violin: Mvt. II
     George Armand, violin;
     Toulouse Chamber Orchestra, Louis Auriacombe, cond.
     Nonesuch H-1066 stereo 71066

Concerto in F Major for Three Violins and Strings: Mvt. II
     Allegro Chamber Orchestra, Jan Tubbs, cond.
     Allegro 3146

TELEMANN, GEORG PHILIPP (Cont.)

Concerto in D Major for Four Violins: Mvt. II
Rudolf Schultz, Willy Kirch, Hans Westphal, Giorgio Silzer
Archive 3109

Concerto in G Major for Four Violins: Mvt. I
Concerto in F Major for Recorder, Bassoon and Strings: Mvts. I, III
Concentus Musicus Wien
Telefunken SAWT-9483

Don Quixote Suite: Awakening of Don Quixote: Mvt. IV
Harry Shulman, oboe
Saidenberg Little Symphony, Saidenberg
American Society 1002

Overture in D Major: Mvt. III
Hamburg Telemann Society Chamber Group, Böttcher, cond.
Archive 3224 stereo ARC 73224

Overture Suite for Two Oboes, Two Horns and Bassoon: Six Mvts.
The Eichendorff Wind Group
Musical Heritage Society MHS-528

Partita in G Major for Recorder and Cintinuo: Siciliana
Affectuoso
Conrod, Recorder
Koch, Tenor-Gamba
Gorvin, Harpsichord
Archive ARC-3043

Paris Quartets (Nos. 1, 4, 6):

Quartet in B Minor:	Triste
	Flatteusement
Quartet in D Major:	Modérément
Quartet in E Minor:	Gracieusement
	Modéré

Frans Brüggen, flute — Quadro Amsterdam
Telefunken AWT 9448-A

Quartet in G Major for Recorder, Oboe, Violin and Continuo: Mvt. II
Quartet in G Major for Transverse Flute, Oboe, Violin and
Continuo: Mvts. I, III
Camarata Instrumentale Hamburg,
Archive ARC-3119

Quintet in G Major: Mvt. II
Ensemble Baroque de Paris
Boite a Musique LD-011

Sonata a quattro in G Major for Flute, Two Viole da Gambe and
Harpsichord: Mvt. III
Schaeffer, flute;
Ulsamer and Haferland, viole da Gamba;
Grebe, harpsichord;
Hamburg Telemann Society Chamber Orchestra
Wilifried Böttcher, cond.
Archive ARC 3224 stereo 73224

Sonata in F Minor for Flute and Continuo: Mvts. I, III
Rampal flute; Veyron-Lacroix, harpsichord
Nonesuch H-1038 stereo 71038

Sonata in A Major for Flute, Oboe and Bassoon: Mvts. I, III
Baroque Ensemble of Paris
Music Guild MG-135

Sonata in A Minor for Oboe and Harpsichord: Mvt. III
Michel Piquet, baroque oboe (c. 1750)
Odyssey 32 16 0050

114

TELEMANN, GEORG PHILIPP (Cont.)

Sonata in C Minor for Oboe and Harpsichord: Affetuoso, Andante,
    Largo, Grave
    Harold Gomberg and Baroque Ensemble
    Columbia ML-6232 stereo MS-6832

Sonata in C Minor for Recorder, Oboe and Harpsichord: Mvt. III
Sonata in E Minor for Recorder, Oboe and Harpsichord: Mvts. I, II
    Alfred Mann, Lois Wann, and Edith Weiss Mann
    Westminster 18589

Sonata in G Major for Viola da Gamba and Continuo: Mvts. I, III
    Johannes Koch, viola da gamba;
    Walter Gerwig, lute;
    Archive 3043

Sonata Polonaise No. 2 for Two Violins and Continuo: Mvts. I, III
    Schneiderhan, Swoboda, Benesch, Holetschek
    Westminster 18031

Suite Concertante in G Minor: Louré
                               Les Irresolutes
    Munich Pro Arte Chamber Orchestra, Kurt Redel, cond.
    Westminster XWN-19042 stereo 17042

Suite in A Minor for Flute and Strings: Mvt. III
    H. J. Möhring, flute;
    Soloists Ensemble of Cologne, Muller-Bruhl, cond.
    Nonesuch H-1078 stereo 71078

Suite in F Major for Two Horns, Two Violins and Continuo: Mvt. III
    Kapp Sinfonietta, Richard Dunn, cond.
    Kapp 9053 stereo 9053-S

Suite in F Major for Four Horns, Two Oboes, and String Orchestra:
    Mvts. IV, VII
    Mainz Chamber Orchestra, Günter Kehr, cond.
    VOX (50) 1080

Suite No. 6 in D Minor for Oboe, Violin and Continuo
    Nuremberg Chamber Music Ensemble
    Archive ARC-3198 stereo 73198

Trio in E Minor for Flute, Oboe and Harpsichord: Mvt. I
    Riessberger, flute; Hertel, oboe;
    Langfort, harpsichord
    Musical Heritage MHS 637-8

Trio in E Major for Flute, Violin and Bassoon:
    Baroque Ensemble of Paris
    Music Guild MG-135

Trio Sonata in B Flat Major for Flute and Harpsichord: Mvt. III
    Rampal, flute; Veyron-Lacroix, harpsichord
    Nonesuch H-1038 stereo 71038

Trio Sonata in E Major for Two Violins, Cello and Harpsichord: Mvt. II
    Scheiderhan, Swoboda, Benesch, Holetschek
    Westminster 18585

Water Music, "Hamburger Ebb and Fluht:" Mvts. I, II, IV, VII
    Schola Cantorum Basiliensis, Wenzinger, cond.
    Archive ARC-3198 stereo 71398

TEMPLETON, ALEC (1905-1963)

Quartet No. 1 for Strings: Mvt. III
    Phoenix String Quartet
    Esoteric 533

115

THOMPSON, RANDALL (1899-   )

Suite for Oboe, Clarinet and Viola: Mvts. II and IV
Berkshire Woodwind Ensemble
Unicorn 1029

Symphony No. 2: Mvt. II
American Recording Society Orchestra, Dean Dixon, cond.
American Recording Society 45

THOMSON, VIRGIL (1896-   )

Louisiana Story, Acadian Songs and Dances: "Sadness"
"Super Sadness"
Little Orchestra Society, Thomas Scherman, cond.
Decca 9616

Three Pictures for Orchestra: "The Seine at Night"
The Philadelphia Orchestra, Virgil Thomson, cond.
Columbia ML-4919

TIPPETT, MICHAEL (1905-   )

Concerto for Double String Orchestras (1939): Mvt. II
Moscow Chamber and Bath Festival Orchestras
Rudolf Barshai, cond.
Angel 35981   stereo S-35981

TITELOUZE, JEAN (1563-1633)

Versets on the Hymn "Ave Maris Stella": Nos. 2 and 3
Andre Marchal, organ
Westminster 18674

TOCH, ERNST (1887-1964)

Quartet No. 7, Opus 70: Mvt. II
Zurich String Quartet
Contemporary M-6005   stereo 8005

Quartet No. 10, Opus 28 (1921): Mvt. II
American Art Quartet
Contemporary M-6008   stereo 8008

Quartet in D Flat Major, Opus 18 (1909) Mvts. I, III
Westwood String Quartet
Contemporary C-6002   stereo 7016

Sonatinetta for Flute, Clarinet and Bassoon: Mvt. II
Murry Panitz, flute; Anthony Gigliotti, clarinet;
Bernard Garfield, bassoon.
Columbia ML-5788

Trio for Strings, Opus 63: Mvt. II
Vienna String Trio
Contemporary M-6005   stereo 8005

TOMASINI, LUIGI (1741-1808)

Suite for Violetta: Lento amabile
Ensemble Marius Casadesus
Westminster 18130

TOMKINS, THOMAS (1572-1656)

Alman
Concentus Musicus
Bach Guild BG-626

TORELLI, GIUSEPPE (1658-1709)

Concerto in D Minor for Strings, Opus 6, No. 10: Mvts. I, III
Copenhagen Societas Musica
Bach Guild 566

TORELLI, GIUSEPPE (Cont.)

Concerti for Violin, Opus 8 — No. 2 in A Minor: Mvt. II
No. 3 in E Major: Mvt. II
No. 9 in E Minor: Mvt. II
No. 12 in D Major: Mvt. II
Reinhold Barchet, Will Beh, violins
Stuttgart Pro Musica String Orchestra, Rolf Reinhardt, cond.
3 Vox DL-113

TOURNEMIRE, CHARLES (1870-1939)

L'Orgue Mystique: Suite No. 18 (in part)
L'Orgue Mystique: Suite No. 35 (in part)
Robert Noehren, organ of St. John's Cathderal, Milwaukee
Lyrichord (7) 171

TURINA, JOAQUIN (1882-1949)

La Oracion del Torero, Opus 34
Hollywood String Quartet
Capitol P-8260

VAINBERG, MOYSEY (1919-   )

Serenade for Orchestra, Opus 47, No. 4: Mvt. III
USSR State Radio Orchestra, Alexander Gauk, cond.
Westminster 18191

VALENTINI, GIUSEPPE (c. 1681-1740)

Concerto for Oboe in C Major: Mvt. II
Silvano Prestini, oboe
Italian Chamber Orchestra, Newell Jenkins, cond.
Haydn Society 9034

VASSILENKO, SERGEY (1872-1956)

Suite on Chinese Themes, Opus 138: Mvt. I
USSR State Radio Orchestra, Alexander Gauk, cond.
Liberty 15001

VAUGHAN WILLIAMS, RALPH (1872-1958)

Chorale Prelude "Rhosymedre"
E. Power Biggs, organ
Columbia ML-4603

Concerto Accademico in D Minor for Violin: Mvt. II
Joseph Fuchs, violin
Zimbler Sinfonietta
Decca 9625

Fantasia on a Theme by Thomas Tallis
New Symphony Orchestra, Anthony Collins, cond.
London CM-9053

Greensleeves
New Symphony Orchestra, Anthony Collins, cond.
London CM-9053

Job (A Masque for Dancing): Dance of the Three Messengers
London Philharmonic Orchestra, Sir Adrian Boult, cond.
Everest 6019 stereo 3019

Lark Ascending
Rafael Druian, violin
Cleveland Sinfonietta, Louis Lane, cond.
Epic LC-3875 stereo BC-1275

Norfolk Rhapsody
Philharmonic Promenade Orchestra, Sir Adrian Boult, cond.
Westminster 18248

VAUGHAN WILLIAMS, RALPH (Cont.)

Symphony No. 2, "London": Mvt. II
London Philharmonic Orchestra, Sir Adrian Boult, cond.
London CM-9052

Symphony No. 3, "Pastoral": Mvts. I, II
London Philharmonic Orchestra, Sir Adrian Boult, cond.
London CM-9063

Symphony No. 5 in D Major: Mvt. III
London Philharmonic Orchestra, Sir Adrian Boult, cond.
London CM-9095

Symphony No. 6 in E Minor: Mvt. IV
London Philharmonic Orchestra, Sir Adrian Boult, cond.
London CM-9096

Symphony No. 7, "Antarctica": Mvt. IV
London Philharmonic Orchestra, Sir Adrian Boult, cond.
London CM-9097

Symphony No. 8 in D Minor: Mvt. III
London Philharmonic Orchestra, Sir Adrian Boult, cond.
London CM-9189   stereo CS-6078

VERACINI, FRANCESCO MARIA (c. 1685-1750)

Largo
Sinfonietta di Roma, Domenico Savino, cond.
Kapp 9044   stereo 9044-S

Concerto in D Major for Violin: Mvt. II
Carroll Glen, violin
Austrian Tonkuenstler Orchestra, Lee Schanenen
Musical Heritage MHS-652

VIERNE, LOUIS (1870-1937)

Symphony No. 2 in E Major for Organ, Opus 20: Mvt. IV
Pierre Cochereau, organ
Oiseay-Lyre OL-50103

VIEUXTEMPS, HENRI (1820-1881)

Concerto in D Minor for Violin, Opus 31: Mvt. II
Zino Francescatti, organ
The Philadelphia Orchestra, Eugene Ormandy, cond.
Columbia ML-5184

VILLA-LOBOS, HEITOR (1887-1959)

Bachianas Brasileiras No. 1: Modinha
Stadium Symphony Orchestra, Leopold Stokowski, cond.
Everest 6116   stereo 3016

Concerto No. 2 for Cello and Orchestra (1955): Molto andante
cantabile
Parisot, cello;
Vienna State Opera Orchestra, Gustav Meier , cond.
Westminster XWN-19037   stereo 17037

Fantasia Concertante for Orchestra of Violoncellos: Mvt. II
The Violoncello Society, Villa-Lobos, cond.
Everest 6024   stereo 3024

Quartet for Flute, Oboe, Clarinet and Bassoon: Mvt. II
Lolya, Kaplan, Neidich, di Carlo
Westminster 18651

Quartet No. 6 in E Major for Strings: Mvt. III
Hollywood String Quartet
Capitol P-8472

118

VIOTTI, GIOVANNI BATTISTA (1755-1824

Concerto No. 3 in A Minor for Violin: Mvt. II
    Guiseppe Prencipe, violin
    Orchestra Rossini di Napoli, Franco Caracciolo, cond.
    London CM-9445 stereo 6445

VISKI, JANOS (1906-1961)

Enigma (symphonic poem) (1939): (in part)
    Hungarian State Concert Orchestra, Gyula Nemeth, cond.
    Mace 9009

VITALI, TOMASO ANTONIO (c. 1665 - ?)

Sonata in B Minor for Two Violins, Cello and Continuo
    Franco Gulli, Cesare Ferraresi, violins
    Giacinto Caramia, cello
    Achille Berruit, organ
    Musica Sacra AMS-46

VIVALDI, ANTONIO (1678-1741)

Concerto in A Minor for Bassoon (P.70): Mvt. II
Concerto in B Flat Major for Bassoon (P.401): Mvt. I
    Virginio Bianchi, bassoon
    Gli Accademici di Milano, Pietro Santi, cond.
    VOX PL-10740

Concerto in E Minor for Bassoon and Strings, (P.137): Mvt. II
    Marco Constantini, bassoon
    I Musici
    Epic SC-6040 stereo BSC-111

Concerto for Bassoon and Strings, Opus 8, No. 6: Mvt. II
    Paul Hongue, bassoon
    Ensemble Instrumental Sinfonio, Jean Witold, cond.
    Period 723

Concerto No. 13 for Bassoon and Strings in C Major: Mvt. II
Concerto No. 14 for Bassoon and Strings in C Minor: Mvt. II
Concerto No. 17 for Bassoon and Strings in C Major: Mvt. II
    Sherman Walt, bassoon; Zimbler Sinfonietta
    Victor LM-2353 stereo LSC-2353

Concerti for Cello and Orchestra (transcriptions by Dallapiccola)
    — in E Minor: Mvts. I and III
    — in A Minor: Mvt. III
    Aldo Parisot, cello
    Baltimore Conservatory Orchestra, Reginald Stewart, cond.
    Counterpoint 568

Concerto in C Minor for Cello and Strings: Mvt. II
    Roger Albin, cello
    Oiseau-Lyre Orchestral Ensemble, Louis de Froment, cond.
    Oiseau-Lyre OL-50124

Concerto in E Minor for Cello and Strings: Mvt. III
    Pierre Fournier, cello
    Stuttgart Chamber Orchestra, Karl Münchinger, cond.
    London LL-687

Concerto in G Major for Cello and Strings: Mvt. II
    Amfitheatrof, Virtuosi di Roma, Renato Fasano, cond.
    Decca 9572

Concerto in F Minor for Two Cellos and Strings: Mvt. II
    Amfitheatrof, Mazzacurati; Virtuosi di Roma, Fasano , cond.
    Decca 9684

Concerto in A Major for Flute (P.77): Mvt. II
    Rampal, flute
    Saar Chamber Orchestra, Karl Ristenpart, cond.
    Epic BC-1293

VIVALDI, ANTONIO (Cont.)

Concerti for Flute, Opus 10:   No. 2 in G Minor — Mvt. II
   No. 4 in G Major — Mvt. II
   No. 5 in F Major — Mvt. II
   No. 6 in G Major — Mvt. II

Concerti for Flute, Opus 44r: No. 2 in A Minor — Mvt. II
   No. 11 in C Major — Mvt. II
   No. 12 in A Minor — Mvt. II

   Gastone Tassinari, flute
   I Musici
   3 Vox VBX-33

Concerto in D Minor for Flute and Strings, P.440: Mvt. II
   Severino Gazzelloni, flute
   I Musici
   Epic SC-6040 stereo BSC-111

Concerto in C Major for Two Flutes and Strings: P.76: Mvt. II
   Severino Gazzelloni, Giovanni Gatti, flutes
   I Musici
   Epic SC-6040 stereo BSC-111

Concerto in A Minor for Oboe and Strings, P.42: Mvt. II
   Leo Driehuys, oboe
   I Musici
   Epic SC-6040 stereo BSC-111

Concerto in D Minor for Oboe, Opus 8, No. 9: Mvt. II
   Pierre Pierlot, oboe
   Ensemble Instrumental Sinfonio, Jean Witold, cond.
   Period 723

Concerto in C Major for Oboe (P.44): Mvt. II
Concerto in C Major for Oboe (P.41): Mvt. II
Concerto in D Major for Oboe (P.187): Mvt. II
Concerto in F Major for Oboe (P.306): Mvt. II
   Alberto Caroldi, oboe
   Gil Accademici di Milano,
   VOX PL-10720

Concerto in G Major for Oboe and Bassoon,
   (Opus 42, No. 3) (P.129): Mvt. II
Concerto in C Major for Two Oboes and Two Clarinets,
   (Opus 47, No. 3) (P.302): Mvt. II
   Gli Accademici di Milano, Piero Santi, cond.
   VOX DL-450

Concerto in C Major for Two Oboes, Two Clarinets and
   Strings, P.73: Mvt. II
Concerto in C Major for Two Oboes, Two Clarinets and
   Strings, P.74: Mvt. II
   Gli Accademici di Milano, Piero Santi, cond.
   Vox DL-450

Concerto Grosso, Opus 8, No. 7: Largo
   Julian Olevshy, violin
   Vienna State Opera Orchestra
   Westminster XWN-18914

Concerto in A Major for Orchestra: Andante molto
   I Musici
   Angel 35087

Concerto in C Major for Orchestra: Mvt. II
   Scarlatti Orchestra of Naples, Thomas Schippers, cond.
   Angel 35335

VIVALDI, ANTONIO (Cont.)

Concerto in C Major for Orchestra, P.87: Mvt. II
Austrian Tonkunstler Orchestra of Vienna
Edgar Seipenbusch, cond.
Musical Heritage Society MHS-588

Concerto in F Major for Orchestra: Mvt. II
Oiseau-Lyre Orchestral Ensemble, Louis de Froment, cond.
Oiseau-Lyre 50073

Concerto in G Minor for Orchestra, Opus 12, No. 12: Mvt. III
Litschauer Chamber Orchestra, Angelo Ephrekian, cond.
Period SPLP-514

Concerto in A Minor for Viola d'Amore: Mvt. II
Renzo Sabatini, viola d'amore
London Chamber Orchestra
London LPS-256

Concerto in D Major for Viola D'Amore, (P.228): Mvt. II
Renzo Sabitini, viola d'amore
Virtuosi di Roma, Renato Fasano, cond.
Certa-Soria 50045

Concerti for Violin, Opus 3 ("L'Estro Armonico")
No. 3 in G Major: Mvt. II
No. 5 in A Minor: Mvt. II
No. 6 in A Minor: Mvt. II
No. 8 in A Minor: Mvt. II
No. 9 in D Major: Mvt. II
No. 11 in D Minor: Mvt. II
No. 12 in E Major: Mvt. II
Jan Tomasow and Willi Baskowski, violins
Vienna State Opera Chamber Orchestra, Mario Rossi, cond.
3—Bach Guild 572/4

Concerti for Violin, Opus 4 ("La Stravanganza")
No. 1 in B Flat: Mvt. II
No. 4 in A Minor: Mvt. II
No. 7 in C Major: Mvt. II
No. 11 in D Major: Mvt. II
Reinhold Barchet, violin
Stuttgart Pro Musica String Orchestra, Rolf Reinhardt, cond.
3-Vox VBX-31

Concerti for Violin, Opus 8 — ("Il Cimento dell'Armonia e dell'Invenzione")
"Spring" No. 1 in E Major: Mvt. II
"Autumn" No. 3 in F Major: Mvt. II
"Winter" No. 4 in F Minor: Mvt. II
No. 6 in E Minor: Mvt. II
No. 9 in D Minor: Mvt. II
No. 11 in D Major: Mvt. II
No. 12 in C Major: Mvt. II
Felix Auo, violin
I Musici
3 - Epci SC-6029

Concerti for Violin, Opus 9 — ("La Cetra")
No. 1 in C Major: Mvt. II
No. 3 in G Minor: Mvt. II
No. 5 in A Minor: Mvt. II
No. 8 in B Minor: Mvt. II
Reinhold Barchet, violin
Stuttgart Pro Musica String Orchestra, Rolf Reinhardt
3-Vox DL-203

VIVALDI, ANTONIO (Cont.)

Concerto in A Major for Violin ("Pisendel"): Mvt. II
  Richard Burgin and Ruth Posselt, violins
  Cambridge Society for Early Music, Erwin Bodky, cond.
  Kapp 9024

Concerto in C Minor for Violin ("Il Sospetto"): Mvt. II
  Arrigo Pellicia, violin
  Virtuosi di Roma, Renato Fasano, cond.
  Decca 9729

Concerto in B Minor for Violin: Mvt. III
  Huguette Fernandez, violin
  Paris Collegium Musicum, Roland Douatte
  Nonesuch H-1018

Concerto in E Major for Violin ("Il Amoroso"): Mvt. II
  Walter Galozzi, violin
  I Musici
  Epic LC-3486   stereo BC-1021

Concerto in E Minor for Violin ("Il Favorito"): Mvt. II
  Roberto Michelucci, violin
  I Musici
  Epic LC-3486   stereo 1021

Concerto in F Major for Violin: Mvt. II
  Remeo Fantuzzi, violin
  Scuolo Veneziann Orchestra, Angelo Ephrikian, cond.
  Stradivari 621

Concerto in G Minor for Violin, Opus 12, No. 1: Mvt. II
  Peter Rybar, violin
  Vienna Symphony Orchestra, Rudolf Moralt, cond.
  Westminster 18718

Concerto for Violin, Opus 12, No. 1 (P.343): Mvt. II
  Kogan, violin
  Moscow Chamber Orchestra, Barshai, cond.
  Monitor MC-2018

Concerto in B Flat Major for Violin, Cello and Strings: Mvt. II
  Virtuosi di Roma, Renato Fasano, cond.
  Decca 9684

Concerto in D Minor for Violin, Organ and Strings: Mvt. II
  Scarlatti Orchestra of Naples, Franco Caracciolo, cond.
  Angel 35254

Concerto in A Minor for Two Violins and Strings: Mvt. II
  Felix Ayo and Roberto Michelucci, violins
  I Musici
  Epic SC-6040   stereo BSC-111

Concerto for Two Violins and Strings — in D Minor: Mvt. II
                                      in C Minor: Mv.t II
                                      in G Minor: Mvt. II
                                      in D Major: Mvt. II
  Isaac Stern and David Oistrakh, violins
  The Philadelphia Orchestra, Eugene Ormandy, cond.
  Columbia ML-5604   stereo MS-6204

Concerto in G Major for Two Violins, Two Cellos and Orchestra: Mvt. II
  George Alès, Robert Gendre, violins
  Roger Albin, André Rémond, cellos
  Oiseau-Lyre Instrumental Ensemble, Louis de Froment, cond.
  Oiseau-Lyre OL-50124

Concerto in F Major for Three Violins and Strings: Andante
  I Musici
  Angel 35088

122

VIVALDI, ANTONIO (Cont.)

Concerto Opus 11, No. 2 ("Il Favorito") (P.106): Mvt. II
    Roberto Michelucci, violin
    I Musici
    Epic LC-3486

Concerto, Opus 35, No. 6 ("L'Amoroso"): Mvt. II
    Felix Ayo, violin
    I Musici
    Epic LC-3486

Concerto in F Major for Two Horns and Strings: (P.302): Mvt. II
    Mainz Chamber Orchestra, Gunter Kehr, cond.
    VOX STDL 501.080

Concerti for Flute, Violin, Bassoon, and Harpsichord:
        In G Minor (F.XII, No. 8): Largo
        In F Major (F.XII, No. 21): Largo
    Gastone Tassinari, flute
    Renato Giangrandi, violin
    Giorgio Semprini, bassoon
    Arlette Eggmann, harpsichord
    Period SPL-755

Concerto in D Minor for Two Violins (P.281): Mvt. II
Concerto in E Minor for Strings (P.127): Mvt. II
    Leclair Instrumental Ensemble, J. F. Paillard, cond.
    Musical Heritage MHS-537

Concerto in G Minor (tomo 103, P. 403): Mvt. II
    Julius Baker, flute
    Eugenia Earle, harpsichord
    Anthony Checchia, bassoon
    Musical Heritage Society MHS-V.1

Concerto in F Major for Three Violins (tomo 88, P. 278): Mvt. II
    New York Sinfonietta, Max Goberman, cond.
    Musical Heritage Society MHS-V.1

Concerto in F Major for viola d'amore (p.286)
    Two Oboes, bassoon, two horns, and figured bass: Mvt. II
    Chamber Group, Max Govermann, cond.
    Musical Heritage Society MHS-V.2

Concerto in D Major for Strings, (P.197): Mvt. II
    New York Sinfonietta, Max Goberman, cond.
    Musical Heritage Society MHS-V.2

Concerto in C Minor for Two Violins and Strings, (P.436): Mvt. II
    Helen Kwawasser and Nadia Koutzen, violins
    New York Sinfonietta, Max Goberman, cond.
    Musical Heritage Society MHS-V.2

Concerto in G Minor, (P.383): Mvt. II
Concerto in C Major (P.54):
    New York Sinfonietta, Max Goverman, cond.
    Musical Heritage Society MHS-V.3

Concerto in D Minor for Violin, (P.310): Largo
    Paul Gershman, violin
    New York Sinfonietta, Max Goberman, cond.
    Musical Heritage Society MHS-V.7

VIVALDI, ANTONIO (Cont.)

Concerto in E Flat for Bassoon(P.342): Mvt. II
    Frank Schwartz, bassoon
Concerto in A Major (P.231): Mvt. II
Concerto in C Major for Oboe (P.50): Mvt. II
    Arthur Krilov, oboe
Concerto in G Minor (P.360): Mvt. II
Sonata in F Major (P.7, No. 4): Mvt. II
    New York Sinfonietta, Max Goberman, cond.
    Musical Heritage Soceity MHS-V.11 and V.6

Concerto in G Major (P. 135): Mvt. II
Concerto in A Major for Viola d'Amore (P.233): Andante
Sonata in C Minor (P.7, No. 1): Mvt. II
    New York Sinfonietta, Max Goberman, cond.
    Musical Heritage Society MHS-V.12 and V.13

Concerto in D Minor (P.280): Mvt. II
Concerto in A Major (P.236): Mvt. II
Concerto in F Major (P.292): Mvt. II
Concerto in G Major for Flute, Oboe and Bassoon (P.402): Mvt. II
Concerto in G Major for Flute, Oboe, Violin and Bassoon (P.105):
    Mvt. II
    New York Sinfonietta, Max Goberman, cond.
    Musical Heritage Society MHS-V.16

Concerto in C Minor (P.427): Mvt. II
Concerto in F Major (P.320): Mvt. II
Concerto in A Minor (P.77): fragment
    New York Sinfonietta, Max Goberman, cond.
    Musical Heritage Society MHS-V.14

Concerto in F Major (P.279): Mvt. II
Concerto in A Major (P.230): Mvt. II
Concerto in B Flat Major (P.406): Mvt. II
Concerto in G Minor (P.359): Mvt. II
Concerto in C Major (P.43): Mvt. II
Concerto in D Major (P.191): Mvt. II
Concerto in D Major (P.206): Mvt. II
    Harry Schulman, oboe
    New York Sinfonietta, Max Goberman, cond.
    Musical Heritage Society MHS-V.17 and V.15

Pastor Fido, Opus 13, Suite: Mvts. II, IV
    Paris Collegium Musicum, Roland Douatte, cond.
    Nonesuch H-1018   stereo 71018

Sinfonia in B Minor ("Al Santo Sepolcro")
    Scarlatti Orchestra of Naples, Thomas Schippers, cond.
    Angel 35335

Sinfonia in G Major: part two
    Hungarian Chamber Orchestra, Vilmos Tátrai, cond.
    Monitor MC-2056   stereo S-2056

Symphony No. 19 in E Major: Mvt. II
    New York Sinfonietta, Max Goberman, cond.
    Musical Heritage Soceity MHS-V.4

Trio in E Minor
    Allegro Chamber Orchestra, Jan Tubbs, cond.
    Allegro 3146

VORISEK, JAN VACLAV (1791-1825)

Symphony in D Major: Mvt. II (in part)
    Prague Chamber Orchestra
    Crossroads 22 16 0007   stereo 22 16 0008

WAGENAAR, BERNARD (1894-   )

Symphony No. 4: Mvt. IV
    Orchestra conducted by Herbert Haefner
    American Recording Society 21

WAGNER, RICHARD (1813-1883)

Adagio for Clarinet and String Quartet
    Alfred Boskovsky, clarinet
    Members of the Vienna Octet
    London CS-6234

Die Meistersinger: Prelude to Act III
    NBC Symphony Orchestra, Arturo Toscanini, cond.
    Victor LM-6020

Parsifal: Prelude to Act I
    Klingsor's Magic Garden
    Good Friday Spell
    The Philadelphia Orchestra, Eugene Ormandy, cond.
    Columbia ML-5080

Tristan and Isolde: Prelude to Act III
    Detroit Symphony Orchestra, Paul Paray, cond.
    Mercury MG-50107   stereo 90107

WALTON, WILLIAM (1902-   )

Concerto for Cello and Orchestra: Mvt. III (Lento only)
    Gregor Piatigorsky, cello
    Boston Symphony Orchestra, Charles Munch, cond.
    Victor LM-2109   stereo LSC-2109

Henry V: "Death of Falstaff"
        "Touch Her Soft Lips and Part"
    Philharmonia String Orchestra, Sir William Walton, cond.
    His Master's Voice C-7635

Henry V: "Death of Falstaff"
        "Touch Her Soft Lips and Part"
    Cleveland Opos Orchestra, Louis Lahe, cond.
    Epic LC-3809

Second Symphony: Mvt. II
    Cleveland Orchestra, Georges Szell, cond.
    Epic LC-3812

String Quartet in A Minor (1947): Mvt. III
    Allegri String Quartet
    Argo RG-329   stereo (S)-329

WARD, JOHN (date of birth unknown—died prior to 1641)

Ayre for Two Bass Viols and Continuo
    Neville Marriner and Peter Gibbs, violins
    Desmond Dupre and Dennis Nesbitt, bass viols
    Thurston Dart, Chamber Organ and Harpsichord
    L'Oiseau-Lyre OL-50133

Fantasia for Four Viols
    Studio der Fruhen Musik
    Concentus Musicus, Wein, cond.
    Telefunken SAWT-9472

WARD, ROBERT (1917-   )

Symphony No. 1 (1941): Mvt. II (in part)
    Vienna Symphony Orchestra, Dean Dixon, cond.
    Desto D-405

Symphony No. 3 (1950): Mvt. II
    Iceland Symphony Orchestra, Igor Buketoff, cond.
    Composers Recordings, Inc. CRI-206

WARLOCK, PETER (1894-1930)

    Capriol Suite: Pavanne' Pieds-en-l'air
        Kapp Sinfonietta, Emanuel Vardi, cond.
        Kapp 9059 stereo 9059-S

    Serenade for Frederick Delius
        Boyd Neel String Orchestra, Boyd Neel, cond.
        London LD-9170

    Serenade for Strings (1921-22)
        Cleveland Sinfonietta, Louis Lane, cond.
        Epic LC-3875 stereo BC-1275

WAXMAN, FRANZ (1906-   )

    Sinfonietta for Strings and Tympani: Mvt. II
        Los Angeles Festival Orchestra, Franz Waxman, cond.
        Decca 9889

WEBER, CARL MARIA VON (1786-1826)

    Quintet for Clarinet in B Flat Major: Mvt. II
        David Glaser, clarinet
        The Kohon Quartet
        Turnabout 34151

WEBERN, ANTON (1883-1945)

    Five Pieces for String Quartet, Opus 5: Nos. 2, 4, 5
        Juilliard String Quartet
        Victor LM-2531 stereo LSC-2531

WEILL, KURT (1900-1950)

    Johnny Johnson (1936): "The Song of the Goddess"
                      "The Song of the Guns"
        MGM Chamber Orchestra, Arthur Winograd, cond.
        MGM 3334

WHITE, ROBERT (? - 1574)

    In Nomine
        The In Nomine Players
        Vanguard-Bach Guild BG-576

WIDOR, CHARLES MARIE (1844-1937)

    Symphony No. 5 in F Minor for Organ: Mvt. IV
        Feike Asma, organ
        Epic LC-3156

    Symphony No. 6 in G Minor for Organ: Mvts. II, III
        Albert Schweitzer, organ
        Columbia ML-5290

    Symphony No. 10 for Organ, Opus 73: Mvt. III
        William Self, organ
        Classic CE-1012

WIENIAWSKI, HENRYK (1835-1880)

    Concerto No. 2 in D Minor for Violin and Orchestra, Opus 22: Romanza
        Heifetz, violin
        RCA Victor Symphony Orchestra, Solomon, cond.
        Victor LM-1913

    Concerto No. 1 for Violin in F Sharp Minor: Mvt. II
        Michael Rabin, violin
        Philharmonia Orchestra, Sir Adrian Boult, cond.
        Angel 35484

WILTON, CHARLES HENRY (c.1750-c.1800)

Trios for Strings — No. 1 in A Major: Mvt. II
No. 3 in C Major: Mvt. II
No. 6 in F Major: Mvt. I
Jean Pougnet, Frederick Riddle, Anthony Pini
Westminster 9034

YARDUMIAN, RICHARD (1917-   )

Armenian Suite: Song
Lullaby
The Philadelphia Orchestra, Eugene Ormandy, cond.
Columbia ML-4991

Cantus Animae et Cordis
The Philadelphia Orchestra, Eugene Ormandy, cond.
Columbia ML-5629 stereo MS-6229

Chorale-Prelude
The Philadelphia Orchestra, Eugene Ormandy, cond.
Columbia ML-5629 stereo MS-6229

Concerto for Violin: Mvt. II
Anshel Brusilow, violin
The Philadelphia Orchestra, Eugene Ormandy, cond.
Columbia ML-6259 MS-6859

Symphony No. 1: Mvt. II
The Philadelphia Orchestra, Eugene Ormandy, cond.
Columbia ML-6259 MS-6859

ZAVATTERI (XVIII cent.)

Overture, "Al Gusto Teatrale": Mvt. II
Sinfonietta di Roma, Domenico Savino, cond.
Kapp 9044 stereo S-9044

ZELENKA, JAN DISMAS (1679-1745)

Sonata No. 4: Mvt. III
Sonata in F Major (No. 5): Mvt. II
Sonata in C Minor (No. 6): Mvt. III
Oboes: Ray Toubman, Wilfred Burkle
Bassoon: John Miller
Continuo: Danile Pinkham, harpsichord
David Carroll, bassoon
Olivia Toubman, cello
Cambridge CRS-1814

ZELTER, K. F. (1758-1832)

Viola Concerto in E Flat Major: Mvt. II
Georg Schmid, Saar Radio Chamber Orchestra, Ristenpart, cond.
Musical Heritage Soceity MHS-740

ZIPOLI, DOMENICO (1688-1726)

Adagio in F Major (Arr. Giovanni)
Pierlot, oboe; Fonteny, cello
J. F. Paillard Chamber Orchestra
Musical Heritage MHS-595

MISCELLANEOUS
Sacred Instrumental Music from Bohemia and Moravia

Agnes von Behmen (XIV Cent.), Rondel zu Ehren det hl.
Wenzeslaus (XV Cent.), Hymne zu Ehren des hl.
Jan Campanus Vodansky, Moette "Rorando caeli"
Kristof Harant z Polzic, Motette "Maria Kron"
Adam Michna z Otradovic, Sech Stucke aus dem "Liuto boemo"
Pavel Joseph Vejvanovsky, Sonata a quattro, (m. oboe)
Josef Seger, Fuga "Hodie Christus natus est"
Bohuslav Matej Cernohorsky, Fuga
Jan Dismas Zelenka, Zwischenspiel aus der Oper su Ehren
        des hl. Wenzeslaus
Jiri Ignac Linek, Sinfonia Pastorale: Mvt. 2
                  Pro Arte Antiqua of Prague (diskantoviola,
                      sopranviola, altviola, tenor viola da gamba,
                      bassviola da gamba, orgelpositiv cembalo,
                      oboe.)
                  Musica Sacra MAS 17

COMPOSER UNKNOWN

Cant del Ocells (arr. Casals)
  Pablo Casals, cello;
  Prades Festival Orchestra
  Columbia ML-4962

Coda de Volpe
  Trio or Recorders
  Nonesuch H-1010

Dance Suite in G Minor: Allemande
                       Gagliarde
                       Sarabande
                       Gavotte
  Philomusica of London, Thurston Dart
  Oiseau Lyre 50174

Daphne
Master Newman's Pavan
  Viols: The Dolmetsch Consort
  Nonesuch HB-3010

Partita: Sarabande — Preludio — Bourree
  Elena Polonske, Harp
  Turnabout TV-4069

Sant Marti del Canigo — Sardana.(arr. Casals)
  Pablo Casals, cello;
  Prades Festival Orchestra
  Columbia ML-4926

Sixteenth Century Pavan (arranged)
  Jean-Pierre Rampal, flute
  Lamoureus Orchestra, Armand Birbaum, cond.
  Phillips PHC 9036

Sonata for Violin and Continuo in C Major: Mvts. I, III
  (An unlabeled work found on Concert Hall H-1523)